CUSTOMIZING
YOUR
VAN

3RD EDITION

BY ALLAN GIRDLER
REVISED BY CARL CAIATI

TAB BOOKS Inc.
Blue Ridge Summit, PA

THIRD EDITION

THIRD PRINTING

Copyright © 1986 by TAB BOOKS Inc.

Printed in the United States of America

Earlier editions © 1975 and © 1983 by TAB BOOKS Inc.

Library of Congress Cataloging in Publication Data

Girdler, Allan.
    Customizing your van.

    Includes index.
    1. Vans—Customizing. I. Caiati, Carl. II. Title.
TL298.G5   1986   629.28'6   85-30368
ISBN 0-8306-0242-9
ISBN 0-8306-2142-3 (pbk.)

    TAB BOOKS Inc. offers software for
    sale. For information and a catalog,
please contact TAB Software Department,
    Blue Ridge Summit, PA 17294-0850.

Questions regarding the content of this book
should be addressed to:

    Reader Inquiry Branch
    TAB BOOKS Inc.
    Blue Ridge Summit, PA 17294-0214

Cover photographs courtesy of Lynn Chevrolet and Buick, Waynesboro, PA.

Contents

Preface to
the Third Edition

Are you interested in purchasing and customizing a van? Do you want to do the work yourself and save a lot of money? If your answer is "yes," then you made your most important initial investment with the purchase of this book. This far-reaching, how-to manual will lay bare all of the tricks of the trade and then some. All projects are within the average layman's reach and in many cases involve only simple everyday tools. Current trends and the newest products are presented, together with how and where to buy them.

There is a new chapter on the new minivans marketed by Volkswagen, Renault, Chrysler, Dodge, Plymouth, Chevrolet, GMC, Ford, and Toyota. Another new chapter covers how to customize the minivans. The chapter on music systems has been updated to include the latest technological sound components for vans. The Appendix lists all the companies that supply van and minivan customizing accessories.

A book of this scope cannot be undertaken alone. I wish to thank first and foremost Allan Girdler, who first conceived and laid out the original book; I undertook only the revision and updating of this manual.

Special thanks to Bob White and Dave Beal of Glastop Inc.; without their cooperation and fine examples of refined custom interior work this book would not be as exciting. Accolades to my dear and long-range buddy, Gary Garrison, a supreme innovator, painter, and customizer; to Bob Leyrer, a special note of gratitude for his dynamic interior design conceptions and workmanship. Douglas Burger, San Juan Capistrano, California, gets a thank you for all of the original photography. Abundant gratitude for John Fennell, Vice President of Badger Airbrush, Franklin Park, Illinois, who can always be relied on to provide assistance, photographs, material, etc. We cannot and should not forget the many quality parts and accessory manufacturers mentioned throughout this book who gave unstinting assistance, and the many van owners and builders who gave me access to their "Show" and "Go" pieces. Last but not least, very special thanks to my extremely pretty and extremely efficient typist, Suzanne Zaralban, who always manages to keep it all together for me. My sincerest gratitude and appreciation to all involved in this project.

Carl Caiati

Chapter 1

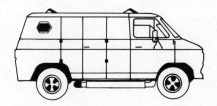

Overview

The men who design, build, and sell vans are good people, and they do good work. They're proud of it. They consider the van as it arrives on the showroom floor to be a finished product, ready to do everything the buyer wants it to do.

No offense to them intended, but this book is for people who don't agree. This book is for people who see a van as a raw material, no matter how complete the option list.

This book is for individuals, people who have their own needs and purposes who are willing to do extra work and spend additional money to convert a vehicle for everybody into a vehicle just for themselves, adapted to serve their needs only. The factory's finished product, then, will be considered here as a starting point.

From that starting point, we will travel in several directions. A van conversion is a personal project, so it follows that each project is different from all others (Fig. 1-1). At the same time, there are guidelines and projects that apply to all or most vans.

This book will not, therefore, tell you what to do to your van. That's up to you. We'll look first at what the factories supply—sizes, drivetrains, options, etc., that are available from the makers, whether the van is new or used.

Then we'll look at individual projects. This will be detailed information for the most part, with step-by-step instructions on how each project was done by the builder and can be done by you. There's overlap here and it's useful. If you plan a van for daily

Fig. 1-1. Every customized van reflects the personality of its owner. The Dodge shown here is a good example of the surfer or cruiser, intended mostly for day tripping.

travel, you will benefit from the camper's knowledge, just as the camper may some day need to know about hauling motorcycles or what-have-you (Fig. 1-2).

When we've seen all of the pieces, so to speak, we'll look at how they've been put together. We have some good examples, vans done (for the most part) by the owners themselves.

This is for inspiration, not limitation. If you don't like what another van owner has done, fine. Take the ideas you like and discard or substitute for the ones you don't like. It's your van.

This book won't tell you everything you may want to know. There's no material on engines, for instance. That is a very important subject, but it is also beyond the scope of this book. If you want to know more, there are other books and shops with far more useful information than we could pack into a chapter here.

Now, then, what are you—the reader and van converter—going to need? Some basic mechanical experience and aptitude, for one thing. This is do-it-yourself material, so it assumes you are inclined to tackle projects rather than farm them out.

The degree of skill varies, naturally, with the complexity of the project. At one end, say the installation of an interior, the converter needs only normal hand tools such as screwdrivers, a sharp knife, and an electric drill, preferably with a screwdriving attachment. Skills are along the lines of drilling holes, splashing on glue, and reading instructions.

Other projects described in this book take more time, skill, and confidence. There is work here for metal cutters, plumbers, electricians, and cabinetmakers. Make note of that last. Some of the carpentry will be simple, some will be difficult, and some will require professional talent.

Some of the results shown will be beyond the skill of an amateur craftsman. The installation of a raised roof is something not even all professionals will do, and to a man, the professionals will discourage you unless you have considerable experience with metalwork. If your project won't be right without a raised roof, farm it out.

Don't let this discourage you. We are looking at converted vans as places to play, live, and travel. Some of the vans in this book are complex. Others are not. How far you go depends on you. If, for example, you don't want to build a cabinet for a sink with an electric pump and stove that uses a fuel cylinder mounted elsewhere in the van, don't worry. You can use portable units that mount and dismount with ease and don't need any extras. If the food gets cooked and the dishes washed, what else matters?

For some of these jobs, you'll need a helper or two. Not just for muscle, although that will come in handy, but there will be times when nothing works as well as an extra pair of hands. If there's a choice of helpers, pick one with the experience you lack. A hus-

Fig. 1-2. Specialized paint makes this offroad hauler unique. Most have simple, open interiors for hauling motorcycles and camping gear.

band who's good with a saw will quickly come to appreciate a wife who knows how to sew and to read patterns.

You're also going to need to know how to follow instructions. Some of them will come with equipment. Most of the projects in this book were intended for performance at home, by the van owner. The firms who supply components for this market know it's likely to be a onetime job; that is, each owner will be installing his first dinette or tape player. The makers try to be as clear as they can. You, the installer, are going to have to trust them, and the best way to do that is to read the instructions first.

You're going to need patience.

And you're going to need confidence. All of the projects in this book have been done. If they've been done, you and I can do them. The first time you put the sawblade through the wall of your pride and joy, you'll be scared. But if you've followed the instructions, every job in this book turns out to be easier than it looks.

Chapter 2

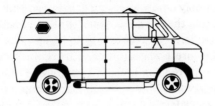

Basics

The ubiquitous van, primarily conceived as a commercial vehicle, has now taken its place among everyday vehicles and has come to the fore against its contemporaries in the recreational and camper field. Since its conception in 1961, the van has metamorphosed in both appearance and size. Longer wheelbases, roomier interiors, improved motive power, and upgraded transmissions have made the van what it is today, based on public demand and approval.

As a custom-designed transportation medium, the van has evolved from the faddish "sin bin" or motel on wheels to a highly utiltarian vehicle. Outdated shag carpeting from floor to walls on the inside has given way to more thought-out, sophisticated decor heightened by the clever use of decorative materials and accessories. Wood paneling, rich upholstery materials, leathers, Naugahyde, and carpeting, used exclusively or in conjuction, serve as standard decorating elements. The selection is governed by individual requirements or tastes.

Although the custom-van furor that took hold in the preliminary stages of the van movement has subsided, new looks and concepts have been inaugurated, turning the modern van into a highly functional and individualized vehicle incorporating practicality with aesthetics. You can assume that the van as we know it today has all but replaced the oversized recreational vehicle in the number one spot, delegating Winnebago and similar oversized motor homes to lesser stature. There are a number of reasons why vans have outshadowed and outsold their big brothers. For one thing, the van's smaller size makes it an ideal everyday vehicle that can serve as a second family car with added fringe benefits. The lady of the house finds the scaled down version of the motor home easier to handle in traffic and simpler to park. She can take it to market, slip it into the same parking space as a car, and fill it with more groceries than would fit in a car. Also, the van is far better on gas than the motor home. In some cases, vans offer gas mileage capabilities equal to or surpassing oversized cars. The vans available today are versatile and can be built and tailored to suit individual needs, a factor not possible with standard automobiles.

The three manufacturers and mass producers of the common stock van are Chevrolet, Dodge, and Ford. GM and Plymouth vans are kinsmen to Chevy and Dodge respectively, with the same configurations save for the labeling. In basic, fundamental areas the big three do not differ much. One emulates the other, all motivated by public demand and requirements, with no manufacturer deviating far from the accepted norm.

Basic, common, integrated options presented by the big three manufacturers are:

- Solid "slab" sides (no windows rearward of the front doors), or windows all around (as in the Chevy Sportvan, Dodge Sportsman, and Ford Club Wagon).
- Short and long wheelbases.
- Load capacity from a few hundred to a few thousand pounds.
- Seating capacities from 2 (commercial vans) to 15 (sport window models).
- Six-cylinder or eight-cylinder V-8 engines.

CHEVROLET VANS

Chevrolet markets three models: the G10, G20, and G30; the numbers designate the payload ranges. The Chevy van is the slab side type, the Sportvan the window type. The short versions have a 110-inch wheelbase; the long version sports a 125-inch wheelbase. In the engine department, Chevy offers a 250-cubic-inch, six-cylinder, in-line engine and the widely used 350-cubic-inch small block V-8 with optional two or four barrel carburetor. Both manual and automatic transmissions are marketed. A myriad of additional options are presented These are two numerous to list but are readily obtainable at Chevy dealers. Chevy vans may be

Fig. 2-1. The Chevy van sports the fewest changes in the last decade—usually localized in the grille and lights (custom paint by Gary Garrison).

ordered with either fold out or sliding doors according to customer selection. In 1979, major changes were made to the dashboard with favorable results. Other changes from year to year have been minimal and localized in the grille and headlight sections. See Fig. 2-1.

DODGE VANS

Dodge, prior to 1979, held the number one spot in van sales, losing ground only when Ford sales surged upward in the opening months of 1978. To compete, Dodge vans underwent a complete styling change culminating in the new 1979 front-end design. The main change took place from the front window pillar forward. The outdated, rounded, sloping nose gave way to an updated, squared-off configuration, which Dodge has maintained to date (Fig. 2-2). Suspension and front subframe were also revamped. The "Tradesman" name on the commercial slab side van was deleted in favor of a "Dodge Vans" nameplate; window vans retained the "Sportsman" nameplate.

As with the competition, Dodge's basic yearly style changes are concentrated in the front grille area. Headlight options include round or rectangular lights depending on trim level. Modifications to the independent suspension on the newer vans include redesigned upper and lower A-arms, coil springs, and tube shocks mounted in the springs. Larger rubber bushings on the suspension control

Fig. 2-2. The pre-1979 Dodge's rounded, sloping nose gave way to a squarer look forward of the windshield.

arms reduce noise, and the coil spring action has been softened. On the older Dodges, front ends would tend to bounce erratically when bumps were encountered. The upgraded new suspension seems to have eradicated this problem. A 1.3-inch wider track up front assists vehicle controllability.

Three engine types fill the motor roster at the Dodge plant. The 225-cubic-inch straight six, the 318-cubic-inch V-8, and the 360-cubic-inch V-8. The usual Dodge transmissions are offered. A lock-up torque converter was introduced into the automatic transmission systems offered for the six cylinder and 318 engines in 1979. The lock-up torque converter, primarily designed for 1978 Chrysler cars, eliminates slippage in high gear, greatly improving fuel economy.

Three Dodge body styles prevail: the short 109-inch wheelbase model; the 127-inch wheelbase model; and the elongated Maxi or super-Maxi van, a stretched out version of the 127-inch wheelbase model that made its debut in 1978. The overall length of the extra long Maxim is a full 220 inches. On the oversize model the side door, optionally available in sliding or swing out mode, had been moved forward 1u inches. In the driving compartment, redesigned engine covers provide more room for the driver and passenger because they are 4 inches shorter and 2 inches narrower.

FORD VANS

Of the big three manufacturers, Ford had undergone the most radical physical styling change. Beginning in 1974, the front was extended to compensate for a more forward mounted engine. A nose or snout was designed to house and accommodate the forward engine installation (Fig. 2-3). This change allowed more room in the driving compartment. This modification, plus improved frame and suspension changes since tested and approved by the van buying public, has made the Ford the most popular and most sought after van.

Fig. 2-3. Ford underwent a complete style change in 1974. A snout houses the engine and keeps it forward of the driving compartment (custom paint by Garrison).

Fig. 2-4. Standard Ford Supervan with typical extended top. This basic approach is favored by recreational and camping vehicle buffs.

In 1978, Ford upgraded their standard transmission package by incorporating overdrive to add to the performance and versatility of the 302-cubic-inch V-8. On the van roster from the E-150 to the E-350, Ford, like its competitors, offers a choice of short and long wheelbase models with sliding or swinging door options. The window version, titles the "Club Wagon," is also marketed with an interesting two-tone paint design treatment that sets it apart from standard and competitive wagons. Top of the Ford van line, the "Superwagon" is the giant in van circles. The superwagon body has been factory extended 2 feet over the original design concept of the already long 138-inch wheelbase Ford van. Though a bit awkward in appearance, the stretched out version has more interior cubic footage than any other model available from any manufacturer. This makes it a recreational converter's dream. Structural mechanical changes from Ford include a new handling package for the smaller vans that features a front stabilizer bar plus heavy-duty front and rear gas shocks, and softer spring rates for the heavy-duty E-350 to make the ride more acceptable. In opposition to its competitors, Ford remains the only van built on a separate frame (Fig. 2-4). The concept seems sound and structurally superior. Engine selection is between the 300-cubic-inch straight six, a real torquer; the 302-cubic-inch V-8; and the 351-cubic-inch V-8 powerhouse. Transmissions include the three-speed overdrive and Cruise-O-Matic with a modified torque converter that reduces transmission gear change slippage. Yearly outer cosmetic changes remain minimal, as with the competition they are mainly concentrated in the grille/headlight area.

Chapter 3

Sources

Although the proliferation of van shops, accessory manufacturers, and custom labor sources has diminished from what it was seven years ago when the van craze was at its height, there are still many sound sources for parts and accessories. The specialized custom van shop is now relegated to a minority status. The scattered few that remain are still going strong primarily because they offer quality workmanship, good service, and readily available parts, materials, and accessories.

Vast changes have manifested themselves in the van industry and the appearance of the vans themselves. These changes has forced van shops to regear their approaches and philosophies, and the major existing van shops can be called upon to provide progressive design as well as the latest in diversifies accessories.

WINDOWS

The most radical change is in window configuration. With larger windows replacing the miniports in popularity, manufacturers are now thinking in terms of bigger and better because the van owner of today wants more functional cruising vehicle with an unobstructed view. The newer bay or picture windows adopted by the vast majority of the vanning set are available in many styles and shapes as illustrated in Chapter 5. Window layout is the first step in van design, and in most cases the windows are the first items purchased and installed.

Many companies specialize in window production. The most prominent and quality-conscious manufacturers are Sketch Forming Corp., Hehr, LeVan, and Elixer. Their products are stocked by a majority of the van accessory and conversion shops. These leading brands are the best and are almost identical in appearance and quality. Some producers may feature distinct or unusual designs that the competition do not have, but the basic "bays or sliders" bear a marked similarity among manufacturers.

Stretch Forming, one of the earliest pioneers in the van movement, is still considered a prime innovator and leader in custom vans and RV window design. Their concepts and workmanship are first rate; their quality, durability, availability, and ease of installation have been proven. The company also makes available an attractive and informative brochure illustrating all of the current trend-setting styles, listing sizes, and installation capabilities. This handy brochure may be obtained by writing to:

> *Stretch Forming Corp.*
> 10870 Talbert Avenue
> Fountain Valley, CA 92708

SUPPLIERS

Most do-it-yourself van buffs who wish to undertake it all may obtain such necessary items as van patterns (interior plans), drappery, drapery hardware, moldings, trim, and fasteners from:

> *Recmar Products*
> 3307 West Castor
> Santa Ana, CA 92704

One dollar will get you Recmar's catalog listing their inventory.

If you live in an outlying or out-of-the-way area with no access to van shops, mail order may be your answer and quite possibly the only source of supply. The larger van supply outlets are usually well stocked and can supply such standby items as seats, windows, flares, grilles, running boards, spoilers, and a host of standard small and large accessories. In most cases, you will have to pay the shipping expenses.

A prominent mail-order source that ships nationally is:

> *Dick Cepek, Inc.*
> 9201 California Avenue
> South Gale, CA 90280

Cepek specializes in van accessories and off-road vehicles and is also a well-known tire dealer. Cepek can supply many of the available items in the heavy-duty line and a wide array of camping and RV accessories.

Sierra Vans
1581 West Wardlow Avenue
Long Beach, CA 90800

Sierra is basically a van conversion house that builds vans on an auto dealer level. They also do private conversions and, as a sideline, sell some heavy-duty convertible beds that the average mail-order house may not stock.

In the northeast, a source of the more common van parts is:

D & A 4-Way
1909 Guilderland Avenue
Schenectady, NY 12306

D & A's big thing is four-wheel drive, but they do supply mail order van supplies. They will send you a catalog for one dollar.

Burnmeister supply is a prominent seat distributor and a sound supplier specializing in all types of van accessories.

Burmeister Supply
1039 East 14 Mile Road
Troy, MI 48084

PERIODICALS AND VAN SHOPS

To discover the latest trend factors and new product lines, consult the pages of the monthly periodicals devoted to vans and van customizing. These periodicals not only provide source material but also give helpful hints and outline building procedures useful to the average do-it-yourselfer. The current magazines found on all nationwide newsstands are *Truckin* and *Vans and Trucks*. Both originate in California and keep abreast of contemporary trends and approaches to custom-van construction. Van clubs are another excellent source of information and can be found nationwide, usually through van or custom magazines that list them by area and address.

The van owner and fabricator who wishes to have his accessories and services at hand must rely on the closest van shop.

Though these may be widely scattered, they are the best source outlets because you can see what you are purchasing. In most cases, you can be assisted by the owner or manager who can best advise and serve you. Van shops that have weathered the fad storm and have remained in business throughout the van movement have done so because they promote quality products and do quality work.

LOCALE AND VAN TRENDS

Locale can also have influence on van trends. Custom showpieces and cruiser vans are most popular in California; radical approaches are apparent in their lavish interiors and wild exteriors. The midwest is strong on camping and RV-type equipment, which incidentally has had much influence on current van trends. This makes today's van a vehicle that stresses functionality and individuality. The owner, however, should have the last word in any design specification governed by individual taste and predilection.

The easiest way to locate the better van shops is by perusing the Yellow Pages of the phone book. Look under "Van Customizing" or "Campers-Equipment, accessories." Some may only serve as retail accessory outlets; some may be inclined toward conversion and custom work as well. In most cases, the "working" shop will be only too glad to see you parts and pieces, while throwing in a little advice and help in order to please and secure you as a customer.

This book can be your most valuable asset and will provide a wealth of information and constructive hints. The projects entailed are within easy reach of even the duffer and can be undertaken with common household tools. Throughout the book, we will deal with various facets of van customizing. Each chapter will be devoted to a different segment of van construction or aesthetic embellishment. As we cover different phases, equipment, etc., we will also provide availability and source data together with personal recommendations geared to assist you in beautifying your van and part-time home-on-wheels.

Chapter 4

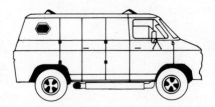

Interiors

A custom interior is the largest—and most visible—single project for a converted van. Every builder's needs and wants are different, so every converted van interior is different. The number and size of projects varies from, say, a new courtesy light to the addition of completely new floor, walls, and ceiling.

We'll spend this chapter dealing with more-or-less complete interiors. The "more-or-less" refers to starting points. Passenger vans come with wall and roof panels and some insulation, while commercial vans are nothing but bare metal, whether the walls have windows or not. As mentioned earlier, there are no kits for doing windowed walls and such a project is difficult. We'll assume that the window vans will be treated only to carpeting, while the closed van will get the complete job.

Today, the trend has been away from completely carpeted interiors. Carpeting is still used on a great many floors, but wall and ceiling decorating approaches favor wood paneling (Fig. 4-1), Naugahyde, and in scattered instances, lush fabrics such as crushed velvets, velours, and woven cloth.

PANELING

Wood paneling is very popular and in wide use because it is attractive, varied, and economical. It is necessary, however, to provide a few pointers on buying paneling.

Most paneling is manufactured in huge, long, pliable rolls four

Fig. 4-1. For the novice interior fabricator, wood paneling is advised. Because it is easy to fit, cut, and install, you can easily cover up paneling mistakes with carpet trim around such areas as corners and edges.

feet wide and hundreds of feet long. By the time the finished product reaches the marketplace, it has been sectioned to 8-foot lengths. You, the consumer, must buy paneling in rigid 4-by-8-foot sheets. Two types of paneling are available: hardboard backed and plywood backed. Hardboard or Masonite-backed panels are rigid and less flexible than plywood types. They also do not hold up under the stress, aging, and vibration of constant driving. Plywood-backed paneling is the way to go. You may pay a little more, but you get a little more.

Two types of glamorous wood finishes are produced; real wood veneer, or the more common, less expensive photoplate surface. In appearance, they differ little. Some of the better photoplates (so called because they are actually a photograph laminated onto a plywood backing) are hard to distinguish from real wood veneer. Photoplate runs from super cheap ($6 a sheet), nonscored to the more expensive super detailed, scored versions selling for $12 to $18 a sheet. Scored photoplate wood contains grooves pressed into the photoplated surface to enhance and more closely simulate a sectioned wood face. Photoplate is readily found at all lumber yards and do-it-yourself home supply outlets and is highly recommended when planning your interior on a budget.

The thickness of paneling should also be considered prior to selection and purchase, be it photoplate or real veneer. The ideal thicknesses are 1/8 inch or 5/32 inch. They are the most flexible and easiest to manage while still providing adequate strength.

For the connoisseur or van owner to whom money is no object, real wood veneers are available with surfaces or authentic black walnut, rosewood, or mahogany. These are available at specialty shops only and are almost never stocked in discount or chain store outlets. Be prepared to put a big dent in your pocketbook if you go the real wood route: real veneer woods go from $70 to $100 a sheet.

To the average person, real wood or photo veneer may be indistinguishable, hence a strong case for the more affordable sheeting. The most discriminating individual will want the real wood because of appearance and upkeep. Scratching or scraping a photoplate panel leaves a permanent blemish. Real wood surfaces can be rubbed out, restained, and touched up. Texturing on real wood has an authenticity that is almost impossible to apply in the manufacturing of photoplate. Time and careful consideration should be applied to the selection of wood paneling.

CARPETING

Everybody needs carpeting. Again, the first step is planning. What will be mounted on the floor? Or through the floor? If your van will have a permanent cabinet or a bed, be sure you have the dimensions before you do any work on the floor. It you'll be mounting a water tank, butane tank, or fuel tank from the floor, check the sizes and drill the holes now, while everything can be easily reached.

Step two of planning involves what's going on the floor. Will kids be sleeping there? Will the floor be a lounging area, or will dirt motorcycles be carried? There are two materials generally used between the metal floor and carpet. Which is chosen depends on what will happen atop the rug (See Fig. 4-2).

Whichever, the first bit of work is to remove everything from the interior: any brackets, the spare tire and jack, even the seats. (Don't worry about that. The seat frames fasten with bolts that go to captive nuts permanently attached to the floor. All you need is a wrench on the top side.)

Sweep or, better still, vacuum the floor. Get down into the crevice between the floorpan and wall. Every speck of dust in the van now will stay there forever, unless you take care.

If you're going to install a four-channel or stereo sound system, string the speaker wire now. Don't attach it yet, just string it. Leave plenty of extra wire on both ends and route it from the dashboard, down the firewall, under the mat between the engine cover and the passenger seat, and across the floor to the left rear corner. Standard practice is to have a rear speaker at each corner, so you need two strands of double wire; that is, one wire from the radio and another for the ground, both in the same insulation. Run both wires up the panel between the left wall and door and extend on wire across the top of the door opening until it dangles down the right rear wall.

The floor is ribbed for strength and to resist vibration. Lay the speaker wires in the valleys. For added insurance, you might want

Fig. 4-2. A novel and functional flooring treatment for the vanner who trucks motorcycles. The floor track and tie-downs can be hidden away by a permanently built-in, hinged floor. When not transporting bikes, the floor section can fold down to completely hide bike securing facilities. This also guards against oil spills that can ruin carpeting.

to tape the wires to the floor, just to be sure they won't move around, get pinched, or be cut when you cover them. The best tape for this is the gray duct tape the racers call "Super Tape." Most hardware and racing supply stores have it, but you'll find the best prices at a plumbing shop. It resists everything and sticks forever. You don't need much, just a strip across the wire every foot or so on the flat surfaces and another strip every time you turn a corner.

Wood-Based Floors

The type of floor covering depends upon floor usage. If the van will be a hauler, with heavy or pointed objects resting on it, the material to use is wood, either 5/8-inch plywood sheeting or particle board.

Plywood has more strength and comes in larger sheets, so it may be easier to fit into the van. Particle board cuts more easily and more smoothly. If you'll have a heavy cabinet bolted to the floor plywood is best. If you won't need to worry about strength, go to particle board.

Either way, measure the floor from behind the seat bolt holes to the body seam about 2 inches in front of the rear-door ledge, and from floor edge to floor edge in a bare van (from side panel to side panel in a van with such panels). One plywood panel should fill the space. If not, or if you're using particle board—which comes in smaller sheets—use as many panels as it takes. No problems here, as they'll be covered later and all of the joints will be straight edges. You won't be working with a jigsaw puzzle—not yet, anyway.

With the basic shape established, you'll need to fit the panels to the floor. Measure the parts that need cutouts: the rear-wheel wells and side door for all vans, and the wall braces for bare vans. For the braces, cut a simple square notch deep enough to let the floorboard slide to the edge of the metal floor. Allow 1/2-inch clearance for the wheel wells. The side-door cut is a bit trickier. Measuring the actual dimensions and cutting a freehand curve at the back works well if you have a good eye for such things. A safer way is to use a piece of heavy cardboard. Lay it over the area, with a good share sticking out. Trace the curve from beneath, cut it, and see how it fits. When the shape is right, transfer it to the wood piece. (*Note:* You've just made your first *template*. You will see this word again.)

The wood panel or panels can now be screwed to the floor. The number of screws isn't vital. Use 1 1/2-inch sheet-metal screws and drill the holes through the wood above the raised ribs of the metal floor. Keep out of the valleys. You could hit the speaker wire, pull the board into a warp, or even strike the van's wiring or fuel line, which is routed under the floor. The screws needn't be too close to the edge of the panel. One screw every 8 inches or so should be more than enough.

One optional step depends on the final covering to be used. With a rug of any kind, the finish of the wood board won't matter. Van converters seldom use vinyl, but the right type of that material can be a good choice, especially if the floor will bear heavy traffic. If you'll be using vinyl, the wood panel must be smooth. Countersink the screwheads, fill the holes with wood putty, and sand the entire surface. You don't need a mirror finish, but every little bump on the wood will show through the vinyl when it's too late to change it.

Padded Floors

For the softer floor—the living room floor, so to speak—the edges of the metal floor should be trimmed with narrow pieces of 5/8-inch particle board (Fig. 4-3). Cut strips about 2 inches wide. Screw one strip across the front of the cargo section, behind the seat locations. Three pieces will go around the side-door opening, then a strip goes down the side floor at the level edge, around the wheel well, back down the side to the rear wall, across the rear door ledge, up the left-hand wall, etc. Don't worry about making

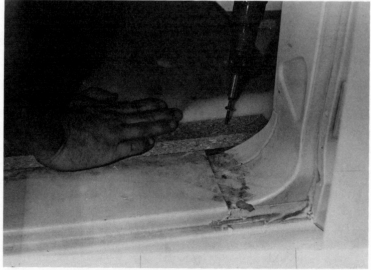

Fig. 4-3. The carpet is held by screws anchored in strips of particle board.

Fig. 4-4. Foam padding for the floor is roughly cut and trimmed, glued into place, and given a final trim. Leave space around the edges.

these strips dovetail together, or even about getting them absolutely straight. They are nothing more than places to fasten carpet. Neither you nor anybody else will ever see them again. Use the same type sheet-metal screw as recommended for the full wood panels and once again fasten the strips to the raised ribs. Put the strips about 2 inches back from the doorsills and 1/2 inch back from the floor and wheel-well edges.

The padding for the soft floor is just that—padding (Fig. 4-4). buy some rolls of 2-inch sponge foam in one of the firmer grades. Any good upholstery shop, or even Sears catalog, can supply it.

The sponge will go between the wood strips. it can be cut with a razor blade, a sharp knife, or even heavy scissors. Cut to make a tidy fit, but the padding need not be perfectly true with the strips. This is something else you'll never see again.

The padding is glued to the metal floor. Contact cement from the hardware store does fine. The pros use sprayers powered by compressed air, but a large paint brush will work for the home builder. Don't be stingy. Slop the glue onto the floor, then onto the bottom side of the padding, let it become tacky and press it into place.

For the fussy craftsman, it's neatest to leave the foam pieces slightly oversize. When the glue has dried and the padding is firmly in place, you can do the final trimming and have the foam tucked tidily away next to the wood strips.

Installation

Most vans use carpet or rug for the floor covering, and the choice is between two types: shag or indoor/outdoor. Shag is shaggy, cheap, and—as the pros say—covers a multitude of mistakes. Indoor/outdoor is much tougher, more expensive, harder to lay, and better suited for rough living. Indoor/outdoor carpet is literally that, a man-made fiber designed to withstand dirt and getting wet. You can sponge it off or even hose it down. It is great for vans that haul things.

There is no best choice here. Which type you use depends on what it will be used for. Usually, although this isn't a rule, the shag rug goes over the foam padding and the indoor/outdoor goes atop the board padding.

Any carpet store will be able to supply whatever rug you pick. They should be willing to advise you, and they may even have some bargains in the form of remnants. A van isn't big, in terms of their business, and the leftovers from somebody's living room may do you very well.

The front of the floor can be carpeted in several ways. The easiest is to have the front edge just in front of the seat mounts, with the carpet tucked beneath the rubber mats that come in commercial or bare vans.

The underlay is ended aft of the seat mounts. There's an option here as well. Factory seat frames are large and bulky. Laying carpet around them is a border. The seats are out of the van at this stage. When you lay the carpet, cut holes over the seat-mount nuts. After the carpet is in place, put the seats back with the standard bolts.

Most custom seats use a flat plate base, drilled to line up with the stock nuts. Heavy steel tubing is welded to the base. The seats have tubing bases, and the seat tube slips over the base tube. If you're using custom seats, put the base in place while you're fitting the front of the carpet. Cut a large hole and the carpet will drop over the tubing. Later, after the rug is finished, slip the seat over the base. The carpet will be a perfect fit.

Wood framing can be extended up to the firewall, but the work exceeds the benefits. Plain carpet will do. Hold it in place at the rear of the front, as it were, and unroll the carpet gradually. When you reach the engine cover, make vertical cuts and keep unrolling as you can. When the curve of the engine cover is passed, trim so the carpet fits snugly against the sides. Then cut along the edge of the carpet between the earlier cuts—the rug will hold the curve. It helps at this point to remove the accelerator pedal and cut a hole for the dimmer switch.

Trim around the bulges over the front wheels. You can't curve carpet to fit and will need separate pieces. When the carpet will lie flat, it's back to the glue pot. No trim pieces are needed here, as the glue will hold the rug by itself, although you might want to invest in more molding strips for the doorsills.

The front-wheel bulges can be covered by cutting one or two pieces of remnant to conform roughly to the wall and the edges of the floor. Apply glue to the rug and metal. Press the rug firmly against the top of the bulge and to the inside wall. Slice the rug where it's above the joint of the side wall and the ends. Press the end pieces into place and wrap the side piece until it meets the ends. Trim off excess.

The rear-wheel wells are done the same way. Cut a rectangle, long enough to go from the gap between well and rug at the front to the edge at the back, and wide enough to go from the joint of wall and well to the gap between well and rug. (Now you know why there should be a gap around the wheel wells.) Glue the rug into place at the top and down the side, tucking the rug into the gap. Slice the rug just above the curve where end meets side and press the ends into place, also tucking the rug into the gap, so that all you can see is rug. Hold the rug against the flat portion of the side and begin to work down, trimming back an inch, pressing the flap into place, trimming again, and pressing again, until you reach the floor.

The above is a simple method and is not too difficult. You'd be surprised, though, at the number of bumps that spring up on a wheel well done this way, and at the ease with which the casual eye can spot the seam.

If you have access to a heavy-duty sewing machine, you can make better covers for the rear walls and front bulges by cutting a small piece of rug to fit each surface, then sewing them together, inside out (Figs. 4-5 and 4-6). Flip it, and you've got a nice little hood sort of cover. When you're sure it fits the way you want, glue it on. The result is worth the effort.

Measure the floor you want to cover. If cabinets, a bolster, bench seats over the wheel wells, or something else will be used, plan to lay carpet around them rather than under them. This makes the components easier to attach.

The rug goes down just like the foam did: cut to a close approximation and test for fit. Then put glue on the top of the foam and the bottom of the carpet and carefully lay it in place. If the rug has a pattern, be sure it's been cut straight and laid in place straight. When the glue has dried, use a carpet knife, X-Acto knife, or sharp razor blades (plural because cutting rug takes the edge off quickly).

Now, the edges. If the van has wall panels, trim the rug flush with them. If the walls are still bare at this point, trim the rug to the edge of the wood strips or wood panel. The rug should be 1/2 inch away from the wheel wells and should overlap past the wood by about 1 inch at the rear and side doors.

The glue will keep the rug in place, generally. Use carpet tacks or staples at the walls, the front of the carpet, and at the strips around the wheel wells.

The method for the doors depends on the rug and the underlay.

Fig. 4-5. Another way to cover a fender well. Foam is cut to shape and glued over the metal. (Note board strips used to secure carpet.)

Fig. 4-6. A quilted vinyl cover (measured and sewn into shape before this step) is pushed into place atop the foam. Glue works here, but the fore and aft edges can be left long and tucked under the carpet.

For shag and particle board strips, the rug should be trimmed long, so it extends about 1 inch past the board. When you're trimming, notch the rug at each side of the opening. Curl it down and staple the rug to the vertical edge of the board. Then trim even with the joining of board and metal.

Indoor/outdoor carpet and plywood can be done with parts from the van manufacturer. Luxury passenger vans have carpet as they come from the factory. They use molding strips, metal shaped in a very shallow sort of "Z"; that is, the outside edge goes flat against the metal floor, then kicks up a bit, then goes inside again, over the rug. The parts department of the maker of your van should be able to get these pieces for you, although it may take a week or so. The strips fasten with short sheet-metal screws. Drill the holes, mount the strips loosely, and trim the rug to extend to the kick in the strip. Then lay the strip over the rug and screw it into place. Neat.

The front of the carpet is more difficult. If it ends in a straight line in front of the seats, the glue will hold and the edge can be tucked under the rubber mats of the passenger compartment.

(Perhaps this is a good place to issue a reminder of sorts—the methods described here and elsewhere are those the professionals use. They don't all use the same methods, naturally, and they don't always agree except to say that this or that technique works best for them. In other words, there is nothing sacred about all of this.)

So much for the floor. Incidentally, the people who sell interior kits offer them with or without carpeting. Lots of buyers take the latter, on grounds that they'll save money by doing this part themselves. The men in the shops are surprised by this. The carpets, they say, are the most difficult part of the kits to do properly.

Carpet isn't the only material you can use. People have done floors with linoleum, vinyl, and even tile. While they surely are durable and easy to clean, they don't have the comfort of carpet. Nor do the insulate the van against noise, which is the major reason people began putting interiors into vans.

Vinyl with padding attached, though, can work fairly well. Armstrong makes a good one, and it can be used by the home builder. The flooring should be particle board, smoothed and with the mounting holes filled. The measuring techniques and the fitting for vinyl are the same as those for indoor/outdoor carpet. (Hint: the vinyl can be shaped and fitted more easily if it's left out in the sun for a couple of hours. Heat makes it softer and more pliable.) Use factory molding strips for the door edges. Don't even try to cover the passenger compartment floor or the wheel wells. The surfaces there have compound curves, and the vinyl cannot be formed into the right shapes.

WALLS AND CEILINGS

Now for the walls and ceiling. Most vans with added-on interiors use panels made of Masonite or beaver board covered with wood-grain paneling. Naugahyde, or rug. (There have been some ultra jobs that used genuine wallpaper, but those are rare and are mostly for show, so we won't get into that.)

The choice of material is a matter of personal preference, and the techniques are similar for them all. There are two ways to do the walls and ceiling.

- Completely homegrown. The builder buys all of the material, cuts his own panels, and attaches them.
- Plans. The builder buys a complete set of plans for his van's interior. He buys all of the material and pieces listed in the plans and uses the drawings as templates.

27

Naturally, the cost of each method varies in direct proportion to the skill and effort required. You can save money starting from scratch. You can save time—and possibly heartbreak—with a plan. Why? Because a van interior is like a jigsaw puzzle. There are lots of pieces and their shapes are irregular. It's tricky to get the shapes right and it's trickier still to make them fit together right.

When the factories design the interior of a passenger van, they have skilled patternmakers and craftsmen measure every place that must be covered. They prepare a complete set of templates. They fit the templates to the van body. They cut the pieces to match the templates, then they see if the production pieces fit. If so, fine. If not, back to the drawing board. The process is complicated, time-consuming, and frustrating. If you do the interior yourself, from scratch, that's what you'll have to do.

This is not to say it can't be done. Many builders have done a job that would impress any expert. On the other hand, the professional conversion shops usually have one or two half-completed interiors waiting to be rescued. The owners tried and found they couldn't do the job.

You are forewarned. If you aren't good with a saber saw, file, and tape measure, don't tackle the walls and ceiling by yourself. There aren't even any pictures in this book to help you because I couldn't find a homegrown interior under construction that was being done well enough to serve as an example.

Rather than detail all of the pieces the homegrown interior will need, I will discuss plans. Homegrown builders can then work backwards, in a sense, with some knowledge of what they will need.

The most important part of the plans kit consists of a complete set of patterns: full-scale drawing of each panel, brace, and wood sheet you'll need for your van. Because they are full sized, you cut out the patterns and then lay them on the paneling or wood, trace the shapes, and cut the various pieces to a perfect fit. The hardest part, then, is done for you. Sets of plans sell for $18 to $20.

With the drawings come a shopping list. For a short, bare van, the builder is told to buy: six 4 × 8-foot sheets of paneling, two 4 × 4-inch fir, 16 feet of 1 × 2-inch fir, 8 feet of 1 × 6-inch knotty pine, a 50-foot roll of foil-backed fiberglass insulation, 1 quart of multipurpose contact cement, 1 pint of wood stain, 13 yards of fabric windlace, and 400 sheet-metal screws.

Because the panels, ribs, boards, etc., must fit as perfectly as possible, you can't drill all of the holes, then insert and tighten all of the screws. Each screw must be done separately: drill, tighten, move, align, drill, tighten, etc.

You'll need one electric drill with a standard chuck and a second drill with a screw-driving attachment and several bits of the right size. Drilling 400 holes is probably a year's work for the average drill and bit. Buy some spares early and avoid aggravation. No professional installer would think of climbing into a van without both a drill and a driver. Their advice is to buy a driving attachment for your own drill, then rent the second drill. You'll need the second drill for at least the weekend, but the $5 or $10 spent on rental will more than make up for the time lost and fatigue you won't suffer.

You have a choice of three wallcovering materials. Wood paneling is just like the stuff you buy at the lumberyard for family rooms and such. The walnut, oak, redwood, or whatever is actually a thin sheet of the good material bonded to a lesser grade of wood backing. Wood paneling is popular for conversions, and the firm that sells the most plans assumes that's what the buyer will want.

Naugahyde sheeting is more expensive and would be pratically impossible to duplicate at home. It's a good grade of material with thin cotton padding glued to the back. It's then stitched into place in a diamond pattern. The machines that do this are complicated and rare. Also, they cost a great deal—so much that even the firms producing interior kits don't have them. They buy rolls of completed material from a still-bigger manufacturer who deals wholesale only and in huge lots. Precision stitching may not be that important to you. If so, a competent upholstery shop could probably make a supply of padded vinyl in your color, to your order.

Naugahyde and padding go over panels of Masonite. It's glued on the flat surface. The vinyl portions are 2 inches oversize all around. This overlap is cut into a wide fringe—narrow at the corners—and the extra portions are wrapped tightly around the back and glued.

Fabric is better than plain wood or vinyl for insulating noise, and it looks inviting and homey. Wood paneling is more durable, and if it gets scratched—as it probably will—a dab of stain will cover that nicely.

The use of rug-covered walls and ceiling was a fad for a time, but a complete enclosure of rug looks odd. It's cheap, though, and it does cover any little mistakes in aligning panels and seams. It is easy to make, too. Construction-grade panels are cut to shape and the carpeting is glued on. In sum, the choice is a matter of personal taste and intent.

The type of material selected makes some differences in assembly. A van is not as square a box as you might think. The walls and roof curve, from front to back and top to bottom.

Masonite will curve to fit. Wood panels are less flexible. For this reason, the wood panels attach to the wood ribs fastened to the van's metal ribs. The inside line is less curved than the outside line, and the middle ribs are thicker than the end ribs, both in the interest of straightening out the curves.

If you're using wood panels, now is the time to trace patterns, cut out the ribs, and put them on the steel ribs on wall and roof. Work carefully, of course. Hold the wood ribs in place and make sure they conform to their mounting surface. If not, a little judicious filing should fix it. The men who sell the patterns say you'll have no trouble if you follow the pattern exactly, and that does seem to be so, if the jobs in progress in their shop are any indication.

There may be some interruptions at this point. Will the van have portholes, vents, or windows? Don't install them yet. It's better to wait until all of the interior panels are in place.

Locate the approximate place where the porthole, vent, or window will be. That depends on your floor plan. It also depends on appearance. For some reason, the place where a rear porthole looks best on a short van often is the place where the factory put one of the ribs. You can remove a section with a cold chisel and hacksaw. Make two cuts and hammer the piece out.

Insulation

Insulation comes next (Fig. 4-7). The most common insulation materials are foam rubber, spray foam, or foil-backed fiberglass. Foam rubber is the least effective of the three. Spray foam must be applied with professional equipment, usually by specialists who deal in spray foam insulation. It is excellent because it gets into every nook and cranny and has the added advantage of soundproofing the van so that outside road noise, rattles, vibrations, etc., are minimized. It is also expensive: be prepared to spend $100 if you go this route. Fiberglass insulation (Fig. 4-8) is widely chosen because it is relatively inexpensive and ready to cut and apply (Fig. 4-9). Exercise care in cutting and trimming fiberglass insulation as it sheds and throws tiny glass particles that have a way of getting under your skin (literally), causing itching and rashes. When considering insulation, the choice of the average do-it-yourselfer should be foam rubber or fiberglass.

Fiberglass sheeting is stocked by any builder's supply house, and the foam comes from upholstery shops, surplus goods, and remnant stores. Try remnant stores first. If they're big, they'll have foam in what's known as polyscrap—bundles of odd shapes and ends, in the 1- or 2-inch thickness you want. The irregular shape doesn't matter. All you'll need to do is trim to fit between the ribs of wall and roof and glue on the foam with the glue you used on the floor.

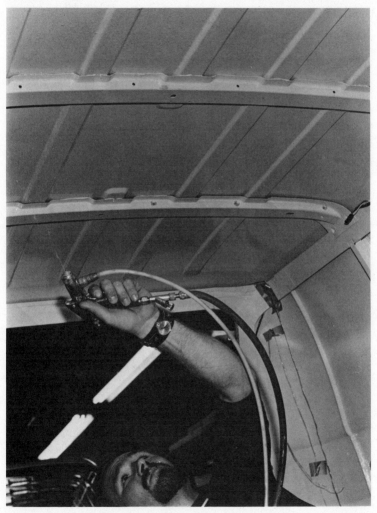

Fig. 4-7. The first step in installing insulation is to spray the metal with glue. If you don't have a spray gun, a brush will do.

Fig. 4-8. Many shops prefer to use fiberglass insulation.

Fig. 4-9. Insulated panels are cut to fit between the ribs, since the ribs are needed for anchoring outer panels.

Installation

The van now should be really stripped. Remove the front door panels and sun visors (if any), the door handles, window cranks, and the courtesy light in the front headliner panel. Unsnap the wires. Put the light aside if you'll use it again, in the trash can if you'll replace it with an accessory light. Either way, don't lose track of the wires themselves. If you'd like a second light in the rear of the van, splice more wire onto the ends you have and run them back along the wall, then across the ceiling. Plan to have the light in the center, but also leave 6 inches or more of extra wire to make the connection later.

The ceiling goes on before the walls. The usual practice is to work from front to back.

The first panel is the hardest. Its leading edge will attach to a metal lip above the windshield. Be very careful here, especially on Dodges, because this lip is narrow and quite close to the roof panel. Most professionals ruefully admit to having put at least one screw through the roof while they were learning. A 1/2-inch screw is best here, and it doesn't hurt to use a tiny strip of Masonite between lip and roof to prevent buckling.

Here's a tip. The factory headliner is ventilated cardboard. The front panel that comes in kits is Masonite and is more difficult to fit properly. The men who do the work say that if it were their van, they'd take the panel that comes in the kit, remove the vinyl covering, and glue that covering over the original factory piece. Punch the standard mounting holes through from the back, and you can use the factory panel with custom covering. There are no new holes and no punctured roof. It makes sense.

We recommend one special tool. Take a 52-inch length of scrap 1- × -2 or large dowel. Cover both ends with foam or cloth. Tape the padding in place. It doesn't matter how this looks. This "helper" wedges the rear of a panel in place while you're working on the front of the panel. You hold the panel up in back, put one end of the stick under the panel, and slide the other end across the floor until it's nearly directly beneath the top end. Leave it there while you're doing the screws in front. Another person would be better, sure, but the stick helper will work well enough.

Anyway, hold the front of the panel *carefully* in place at the center, drill the hole, insert and tighten the screw. Move out from here along the front. Eight inches is the standard distance between screws, but this isn't critical and measuring takes more time than it's worth. A quicker method is to use the span of your own hand:

put your index finger on the screw just installed, spread your hand along the edge being fastened, and drill the next hole where your thumb hits the panel. (Move your thumb first, of course.) This will result in equal spacing between all screws.

With that done, move the rear of the first panel. Before you fasten it, reach in and get the wires for the courtesy light. Poke them through the hole in the panel.

At this point, the wood and Naugahyde methods begin again to differ. The wood panels usually don't meet at the ribs, nor do they need to. There must be some sort of joint. One way to cover the seam is with a thin strip of paneling. Short screws will hold the strip in place.

Less noticeable are seams filled with plastic strips known in the trade as *T-Bar*. Wholesale or retail van equipment stores should have the stuff. It comes in 10-foot lengths and can be easily cut to fit. T-Bar is so called because it's shaped like a Gothic T. There's a wide crossbar at the top and a narrow one at the bottom. The edges of each panel slot into the notches formed by these bars. The wide bar faces the outside and covers the joining of the panels. If that's too much, you can simply sand and stain the edges of the panels and put them close together.

Naugahyde-covered headliner (and wall) panels are installed pretty much the same way, except that they attach to the ribs of the roof and meet each other at the ribs. The rear edge of the first panel should cover half the rib. Peel back the upholstery and lay it over the rest of the rib. Drill and fasten the screws. Lay the front of the second panel against the rear half of the rib, squeezing the loose edge of Naugahyde in the process. Make sure the panel is aligned properly and fasten the front edge. The flap of material serves to cover the gap, while not being so thick as to make a noticeable ridge.

The third panel will go up the same way. A short van takes three panels, a longer van needs four.

The front-door panels are next. First, roll up the windows. Don't forget this, or you may drill a hole in the glass or crack it. The door panels, whether pattern or homemade, should by this time have holes cut for the handles and window cranks. Hold the panel in place, drill, and install on screw at any corner. Position is most important here, so it pays to put the next screw in the corner directly opposite, followed by the other two corners. After that, with the panel exactly where it should be, put two or three screws along each edge.

The same installation procedures are used for wall panels of any type. Install the left-side panels, the side-door panel or panels, the rear-door panels, and the right-hand panels on either side of the side door.

Wood panel lacks a clean edge. You can sand and stain the edges, but for better appearance at the outside edges, many shops use windlace. It is a fabric-covered rope, of sorts. Like fender welt, there's a flat edge that tucks under the panel and a rounded portion that shows. Tuck the flat part under the panel as you fasten the panel down. You don't need to do that at every seam, but it gives the edges at the doors a finished look.

Before you do the rear-corner panels—the ones between the doors and the side walls—be sure to feed the speaker wires through holes where you'll fasten the radio speakers later. The exact location doesn't matter, but take care to have both speakers at the same height.

The final panels are the small, thin pieces that go over the doors. With the pattern kit and wood panels, you'll need kickboards. The wood panels aren't supposed to reach the floor. There will be a space of a few inches. Cut lengths of 1-×-2 to fit horizontally between the wall ribs. Screw them to the bottom of the wall panels and attach the kickboards to these braces. The men who designed the pattern kits say it's good to have this extra strength where the panels are likely to be kicked or have heavy and sharp objects banged against them. See Fig. 4-10.

PLANS AND KITS

At one time, custom prefab interior kits were the rage, but because of lack of interest they are now obsolete. The more sophisticated customizer of today chooses from an untold number of fabrics, materials, and design innovations. The custom prefab kit buyer was tied into one or two interior styles—one or two fabric types that would make a typical and dully repetitive interior.

Commercial plans and blueprints, however, are still popular because no matter what materials are used, the basic panel backing cutout configurations remain the same. Traceable blueprints are available through most van outlets for the three basic Ford, Chevy, and Dodge vans. If you can obtain plans once marketed by T & H Van Works, you will find them easy to work with. Your local van shop may help you fabricate panel templates by allowing you to trace out master templates (if the owner is gracious and generous). If you are a good customer, he may let you do this.

Fig. 4-10. A simple but effective consolidation of space. Seating is tucked against the driver's side wall. Walls are Formica paneling, custom-fabricated divan is Naugahyde trimmed in imitation leopard skin.

The materials and decor chosen is up to each individual. If you like Naugahyde, it can be obtained from a local upholstery supplier. When constructing Naugahyde panel sections, you must remember that the Naugahyde must be backed with foam (1/2 to 3/4 inch), especially when a button tuft affect is desired. The foam is attached

Fig. 4-11. Typical sectioned off van interior. (A) An access doorway is cut in the wall. The clever use of an Indian tapestry draped over entrance assures privacy.

to the woodbacking-mounted panel, then the Naugahyde covering is stretched over the panel board. You have an easy way out here. Prefabbed Naugahyde panel materials are available with simulated buttons and stitching impressed onto the surface. The materials, in a wide variety of surface styles, are prebacked with foam and extremely easy to cut down, glue, or secure to a wood sheathed van interior. The prefab Naugahyde comes in 4-foot-wide rolls, and

Fig. 4-11. (B) A view of rear compartment from back of van. Tapestry covered entrance is at rear. Rear compartment simulates western bunk sleeping facilities.

you can probably obtain it from the better established van shops.

Crushed velvets, standard velvets, and other fabrics are treated like Naugahyde when constructing panels. Remember to use upholstery grade materials, as they are stronger and wear better than materials obtained in a common fabric shop. Upholstery supply outlets or your local van shop can help you. If your local van shop dealer in interior fabrication, he has a source for all of the aforementioned materials. If he is willing, he can save you a lot of footwork and headwork. Prepare to pay a little extra for the materials though, as the dealer should have some compensation for the service he provides you.

SECTIONING

Sectioning off van interiors is popular with some van buffs. This can serve to turn the interior into two rooms or allow a format containing a separate section for privacy or sleeping quarters. Some folks will section off the front driving compartment of the van so that the back section will have a homier, apartment-type atmosphere.

A common sectioning motif is shown in Figs. 4-11A and 4-11B.

Fig. 4-12. An op-art approach to console styling in the Badger Star Bus, designed by Bob Leyrer. He also did the immaculate construction work.

A wall section was erected about 6 feet from the back of the van with an access portal to the sleeping facilities behind. Walls and trim conform to the western theme and atmosphere of the interior. The exterior of this van, which follows through in western flavoring, can be studied in Chapter 22.

Unique console fabrication and refrigerator installment puts the Badger Star Bus's interior (Fig. 4-12) way up in the show custom class. Note ceiling-mounted, sculptured mirror effect. Mirror sections laid adjacent to each other glorify the contoured base. Console is authentic Brazilian rosewood. Plastic tubes glow and radiate blue when bulbs hidden away under the base are turned on. Other views and photos of the Badger Star Bus can also be studied in our "show and go" section.

The closing pages of this chapter depict standard as well as

Fig. 4-13. This photo shows how the front driving compartment of this nearly completed 1964 Chevy van was sectioned off with chromed plastic tubing and custom planter bases (design and construction by Bob Leyrer).

Fig. 4-14. Another method of sectioning off—back section features contour couch (interior by Vandango).

sophisticated special design formulations (Figs. 4-13 through 4-15). Their inclusion may help stimulate the do-it-yourselfer while supplying some innovative ideas that can be applied or revamped to suit particular needs and desires. Chapter 22 will also provide some helpful hints and ideas.

Fig. 4-15. A functional yet decorative recreational vehicle interior (courtesy Glastop, Inc.).

Chapter 5

Windows and Ports

To cater to public taste when custom vans were in their infancy, the major window manufacturers concentrated on small port design. The first ports were round and 12 to 14 inches in diameter. Round ports soon gave way to more creative shapes, and a variety of sizes and designs (Fig. 5-1) hit the market in a wave: triangles, hearts, parallelograms, cat's-eyes, trapezoids, gemstones, and free form all became the rage, with selection instituted by personal taste. Picture windows were also available but did not create a great furor because the early vans, basically "motels on wheels," stressed privacy. Large exterior side areas were also needed to exhibit lavish abstract designs and wild murals, very popular in the early days.

As van design progressed, more and more consideration was given to functional motifs. The van as we know it in its contemporary garb has evolved into a travel and utilitarian vehicle more closely related to the RV than the original sin bin. Outer cosmetics still can be garish and wild, but they are formulated to work in conjunction with bigger windows used singly, in tandem, or in groups that sometimes grace complete sides of the van.

Bay windows are the hot setup. Available in square, rectangular, horizontal, and vertical configurations, they mount in the same fashion as the smaller ports. They must be carefully and selectively placed so that strengthening ribs are not excessively cut, thereby weakening the van's structure. Whenever possible they are mounted between the ribs. If, for design purposes, it is necessary to remove one or two ribs from each side for proper window placement, do so carefully. It can be done but should be avoided whenever possible.

Actually, window installation is a snap: cutting the opening for window insertion is the hardest part and one where the novice experiences timidity. If care is exercised, the job can be as simple as cutting an opening in a sheet of wood. Measurement is the most critical factor, and most window manufacturers simplify this by supplying templates to make the job easier. Cutting the opening too small can be remedied, but an overlarge opening can either ruin the van, making it necessary to undergo major body shop repair, or make the window too loose for proper sealing (Fig. 5-2).

If possible, the inner walls should be in place because all van windows mount telescopically with an inner and outer flange or lip. In addition to the window and mounting flange, some of the better windows supply trim rings to add to the inside appearance of the mounted window. Once the mounting screws are inserted from the inside, the window is securely held in place by the peripheral lips creating a sandwich effect between the interior wall or paneling and the outside van skin.

For cutting the window access holes, the most accepted tools are the jigsaw, nibbler, air chisel, or air shears. The jigsaw may be the most feasible and economical tool for the novice. Make sure that metal cutting blades are used and be prepared to break a few in the process. The nibbler cuts by chipping away increments of metal in a line guided by a steady hand. The air chisel is basically a heavy-duty body shop tool that requires more discriminating expertise. Air shears are like scissors and cut quickly and well. (It must be understood that air cutters must be used in conjunction with an air compressor to power the tool.)

First, the area to be cut out must be outlined. A grease pencil is ideal for this. Trace around the provided or fabricated template. An access hole of about a 1/2 inch is then drilled somewhere along the traced line on the inner side of the proposed opening line. This will allow tip insertion of the cutting tool selected for the job. Cut carefully without applying excessive pressure or you may buckle or crimp the edges of the cutout. Once the outer opening has been cut in the van skin, it can be used as a guide for a saber or jigsaw to cut out the inner wall panel. This can be done from the outside through the previously cut opening. Dimensions of the inside wall are not as critical as on the van skin because the window is maintained snugly in place in the van's wall metal. The inner-mounting,

TearDrop

Parallelogram

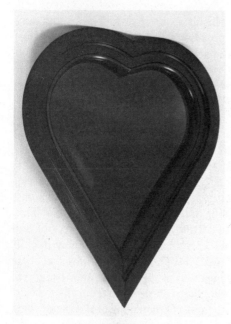

Heart

Fig. 5-1. A number of distinctively shaped small custom
ports are still available from
the stretch Forming Corp.

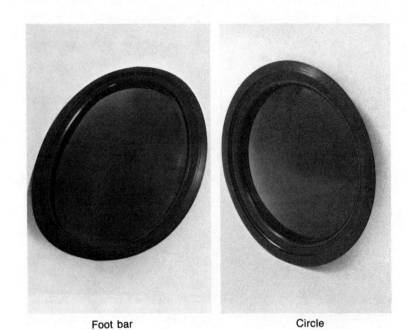

Foot bar

Circle

Gemstone

45

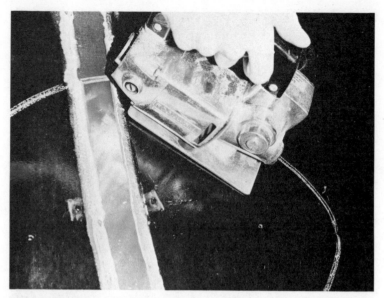

Fig. 5-2. After the window template shape is traced on the van and a 1/2-inch access hole is drilled at one point along the line, the window opening is cut with a jigsaw.

Fig. 5-3. Holes are drilled from the outside opening to the inside van paneling as guides for window location. The window template is then positioned within the guide holes and traced. Inner window opening is cut as shown.

Fig. 5-4. The completed cutout.

Fig. 5-5. After preliminary fitting, trim and fit corrections can be made with an air scissor.

47

window securing lip will compensate for minor inner cutout discrepancies. The two openings should be parallel as closely as possible with the exact window location placement governed by the opening in the van's side (Figs. 5-3 and 5-4).

Finish trimming may be necessary to ensure proper placement and fit within the inner and outer walls. Exercise extreme care in

Fig. 5-6. View from outside of van. Inner trim and securing frame is fit into paneling.

Fig. 5-7. View from inside van. A spacer block is added between paneling and van walls to prevent panel and wall buckling when inner trim ring is tightened against the outside window frame.

the overall operation from the preliminary measurement to the final cutting. Play it safe, and remember it is better to undercut than overcut. A too tight opening may be further enlarged or trimmed. If too much window area is cut away, it cannot be put back. See Fig. 5-5.

Fig. 5-8. Window is affixed and pressed in from the outside. Prior to putting in outer window piece, sealing putty is placed around the flange to insure against water leaks.

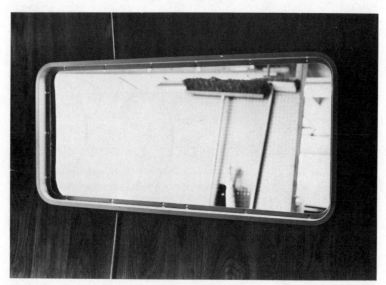

Fig. 5-9. The inner trim ring is secured against the outer window frame with steel screws (usually supplied with windows), and the project is complete.

Horizontal side
bay

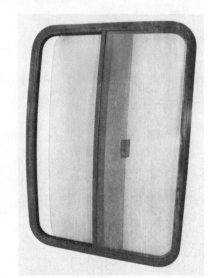

Side bay

Horizontal
slider

Fig. 5-10. Some popular bay window types (courtesy Stretch Forming Corp.).

51

Vista tee short

Vista tee
horizontal

Oval

Fig. 5-10. (Continued from page 51.)

Fig. 5-11. Outer window shades are popular and desirabie, both for keeping sun out and for general privacy.

Shown in Figs. 5-6 through 5-9 is a step-by-step, typical installation of a large window. The window is a horizontal bay or picture window. The construction work was undertaken at Glastop Inc., Pompano Beach, Florida, one of the country's leading van and RV converters specializing in show and go vans. Figure 5-10 shows the various types of windows and ports currently marketed for vans and campers. Figures 5-11 and 5-12 show two vans on which custom window treatments have been expertly used to enhance the overall appearance of the vehicles.

Fig. 5-12. A commonly accepted window installation using small, dual bays.

Chapter 6

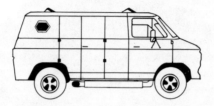

Roof Vents

A roof vent is a handy thing to have in the back of your van—whether the van has windows or solid walls. First, the vent serves as a skylight. It makes the inside brighter and breaks up the monotony of the ceiling. It also helps people—and there are some—who find the van gives them feelings of being trapped.

Perhaps more important and useful is the flow of air. Roof vents usually go in the rear center of the roof. They are thus part of a flat surface running parallel with the flow of air. Aerodynamics works for us here. The rear portion of such a surface develops what's known as negative pressure, meaning that air tends to be pulled away from the surface. If you cut a hole in the surface, which is pretty much what you do when you install a vent, then the air moving over the roof will create a draft, and the vent will cause stale air to be pulled from the interior. Up front, of course, the windows let fresh air in. You have fresh air with no effort, no electric fans, and no buffeting.

Vents are virtually standard equipment nowadays. Like portholes, they can be found at any van or RV store worthy of the name.

INSTALLATION

Installation of a vent is like that of portholes. Much of what follows, then, will be repetition of the preceding chapter. But there are some differences, at least one of major import, so if both chapters apply to your van, read them both.

Choosing the vent shouldn't be a problem. There is one shape: square. There are different features in that some vents open and close with cranks, some with chain. There is a choice of clear or dark material for the translucent dome. These choices are mostly a matter of money, and taste, and need not be involved with the installation.

Where should the vent go? With Dodges, the factory has settled that question for the owner. For the past few model years, ever since vans became recreational vehicles and Dodge set out to capture the lion's share of the market. Dodge vans have been built with a flat, square section in the rear center of the roof. Thoughtful of them, as vans have ribbed roofs for extra strength and resistance to flexing. If you have a Dodge, put the vent where the flat space is. If not, anyplace in the center of the roof, 1 foot or so from the rear edge, will do fine. Just make sure it's far enough forward to be away from where the roof begins to curve down. You want the surface to be as flat as possible.

It's best to have this position located before you install the paneling on the ceiling. You can save some insulation, for one thing, and for another you can be sure the rear courtesy light (if there is one) doesn't have its wire where the vent will go. At the same time, it's easier to panel the ceiling completely and cut the second hole when it's time for the vent.

Vents come as one large assembled unit, with the frame, the hinge, and the movable panel and mechanism all together. There's an inside frame, but we don't have to worry about that yet.

The lower portion of the vent is called a *hat section*. It has a vertical square that extends down past the metal roof to the inside paneling and a horizontal section that lies against the roof. Before the hole can be cut, you need a template. Take a large square of thin plywood or Masonite (or any stiff material, actually. Heavy cardboard can be used). Lay the vent on the board and trace the outline.

Use extra caution at this point. The roof vent will only work if the opening and hinge are in the correct position: *hinge in front, widest portion of the opening in back*. These instructions will be repeated, but then, it bears repeating. With the closed side leading, the wind will flow in the desired direction. Put the vent in backwards, or even sideways, and the force of the air flowing over the roof at highway speed will rip the thing apart.

The vent is supposed to be perfectly square. In theory, you shouldn't need to worry about which side of the template is which.

But the home converter is doing this job for the first and only time. There may be some errors. The shape of the installation hole is being transmitted from the actual part, to a sheet of something, to the metal roof, with cutting in between. Errors can crop up in transmission. The closer you can be to the final product when you begin, the better.

Let the side with the hinge be the front side of the template. Mark it as such.

That taken care of, put the vent aside and cut out the hole in the sheet. Check to be sure the vent will fit smoothly inside the hole. If the fit is correct, that part is done. If not, make whatever minor corrections are needed. If you can't fit it with a few licks of the file, do it again.

The template itself, the square piece you cut from the bigger square, should be marked as to front and top. Draw a diagonal line across the template and drill two holes equidistant along the line.

Put the template on the roof, exactly where you want the vent to be. Mark the template's front and top. Make sure the square is aligned squarely with the roof ribs and trace the template's outline on the metal. Mark where the holes are.

Remove the template and drill the two holes. A 1/4-inch hole will be fine. Use a long bit and drill through both the metal and the inside panel.

Push two long bolts through the holes. Take the template inside the van and push it onto the bolts. It helps to have a helper for this, although it can be done solo if necessary. Be sure the template is in the right position with the front edge in front and the surface that was on top now against the interior panel.

The template should now be directly below the markings on the top of the roof. Trace the outline on the interior panel. Use a grease pencil if the paneling is light or chalk if the wood or Naugahyde is so dark as to make a black line hard to see.

Take the template away. Back to the roof. (It's a bit late to mention this, but when you're working on the roof, it's good insurance to kneel, walk, lean, etc., against an old blanket to protect the paint.)

Cut the outlined hole with power auger or saber saw (using a fine metal blade if the latter.) Check the operations shown in Figs. 6-1 and 6-2. Again, the actual performance of the task isn't as hard as the novice may scare himself into thinking.

The vent will go into a flat surface, exposed to rain. Further, Chevrolet and Ford roofs are ribbed, so the vents for those makes

Fig. 6-1. Mark the size and location for the roof vent with a template. Cut out the hole with a saber saw.

won't be on a completely smooth surface. It will help, by the way, to have the side edges of the vent lie on raised portions of the roof (Fig. 6-3). Usually this happens, as the makers of vents are aware

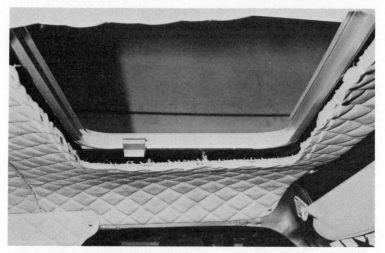

Fig. 6-2. Saw blade should be long enough to cut the headliner panel at the same time. This is easier than trying to make two separate cuts match up. (Hole shown is for sunroof installation.)

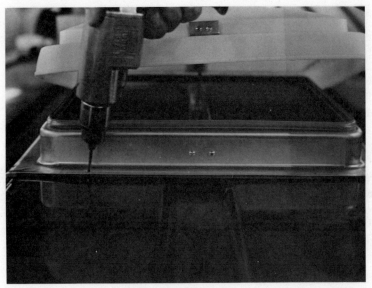

Fig. 6-3. The vent can be dropped into the hole over strips of gum tape. Mounting holes are drilled in the roof using guide holes in the vent frames as pilots.

of the problem. If it doesn't, you can live with it. But try to get a vent with a width that works out this way.

Care must be taken to avoid leaks. you need a seal of some sort. The usual solution here is called *gum tape*. It's puttylike material that comes in strips of what looks like child's modeling clay or caulking compound, about 1/2 inch wide, 1/8 inch thick, backed by masking tape.

Van roofs aren't completely flat, as mentioned, while the frame of the vent is as flat as mass production can make it. There is, therefore, going to be some slight gap between roof and frame. The gum tape fills this gap.

Before it's applied, though, you need to know how much you need. With the paper backing in place, cut strips of tape and lay them around the perimeter of the hole. Lower the vent into the hole and let it rest—lightly—on the tape. If there are places where you can see daylight between roof and frame, that's a place that needs another layer. If the mounting surface is wide enough for two widths of tape, or even one and a half, use them. You can trim off the excess later, and it's better to use too much than not enough.

When you know how much tape is needed where, peel off the paper backing and put the gum down, this time for good. Now drop

Fig. 6-4. Be sure that the hinged end of the vent faces forward. When the vent is open, the wind won't tear it off.

the vent into place, also for good. Make sure the hinge is in front! See Fig. 6-4.

The vent is held to the roof panel by rows of sheet metal screws. Usually the proper screws are included in the package. If not, buy

Fig. 6-5. Vent attaches to the metal roof. An inside frame is attached to the headliner with self-tapping screws.

screws just large enough to go through the holes already drilled in the frame, and long enough to go through the holes and thread into the roof without going too far through it.

The fit of vent and hole should be close enough so you needn't worry about alignment. Even so, drill the first hole at one corner and insert the screw. Move to the diagonally opposite corner, and

Fig. 6-6. The finished project from inside the van. The vent opens and closes with a little crank.

Fig. 6-7. The newest roof vent to gain popularity is the electric fan type. It is installed in the same way as the standard vent.

so on, until all holes are drilled and all screws in place. Now you can begin to tighten, working across the square and never tightening one screw too much tighter than the others. You want to draw

Fig. 6-8. Though not primarily a roof vent, this mini-sunroof vent serves the same purpose while adding a decorative touch to the roof (manufactured by Stretch Forming Corp.).

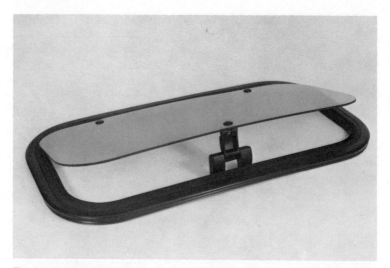

Fig. 6-9. Another larger sunroof by Stretch Forming Corp. is commonly mounted over the driver's compartment. It provides excellent air circulation (courtesy Stretch Forming Corp.).

the vent down against the roof smoothly and evenly to avoid warping or bending the roof or frame. When all of the screws are tight, use a pocket knife to trim away the gum that was squeezed out as the vent was pulled down. A pocket knife, or even table knife, is good here because you don't need a sharp edge and you want to avoid scratching the paint.

Fig. 6-10. The electric vent contains a motor/fan arrangement that improves circulation. This underside view illustrates how the necessary wiring is secured against the insulation prior to installing ceiling paneling (courtesy Glastop Inc.).

Inside, the sides of the hat section should extend to the interior panel or just above that point. Fine. The vent package includes an inside frame, usually four lengths of anodized metal with ends cut at 45 degrees and with a screw hole at each end (Fig. 6-5). The strips fit together, with the vertical edge meeting the vent frame and the horizontal edge lying against the interior panel. The ends overlap, so you simply hold the ends in place while drilling into the panel, then use a short screw to fasten the strips. You're done (Fig. 6-6). Test the vent mechanism and you're ready for fresh air.

FAN VENTS AND SUNROOFS

Two of the newest trends in roof ventilation are the electric fan roof vent (Fig. 6-7) and the sunroof (Figs. 6-8 and 6-9).

The electric fan vent has a motor-driven fan that provides better air circulation for the van. It is connected to the van's electrical system in the same way that any electrical add-on system is attached. A typical installation is shown in Fig. 6-10.

Chapter 7

Stoves

There is to stoves an aspect of being between the proverbial rock and hard place. On the one hand, everybody eats, so if you'll be living or camping in a van, it's nice to have a stove around the rig.

On the other hand, cooking and cooking materials are dangerous. Experience has persuaded many states to pass laws governing stoves in vehicles. These laws involve ventilation of fumes and leaks from pipes, tubing, valves, etc.

The installation of a stove in a van is not a casual thing. The builder's first step is to check into the laws of his state of residence. California, for example, won't permit a stove in a van unless there is more than stock headroom. This means no permanent stove unless the van has a raised roof. Federal parks won't admit a van unless that van has a state permit. Look up the laws in your state.

Assuming the laws are understood and can be complied with, there are three types of stoves generally used in vans. The first is the standard sort of conversion, being a shallow tray with valves and two or three burners. These usually burn butane, either from a separate tank mounted on the van chassis or from a bottle of butane that attaches to the stove framework.

The next step is a module. These are new; in fact, at this writing I know of only one company producing module stoves. It might be better to call them modular galleys as they come with stove, sink, and icebox in one unit. The module is a fiberglass cabinet with the appliances mounted in it. The entire rig can be lifted in and out of the van, which makes it a camping stove, the builders say, and thus not subject to state laws controlling permanent stoves.

The third type is a camping stove like the one you'd haul into the woods. These stoves are compact—no more than two burners— with a fuel bottle that plugs in. They are the cheapest and handiest and require no installation at all. They are exempt from the in-van stove laws.

CABINETWORK

Now for the details. Standard conversion stoves are made by the companies that make the other appliances in this field. They can be bought through an RV store or from the various mail-order houses listed earlier. Both the across-the-counter and the mail-order stores will have complete dimensions for whatever model you pick. Length and width are obvious. Less obvious may be depth—the distance the stove extends below the mounting surface. This is vital because the stove unit comes just as is. You'll have to build a cabinet for it, and it makes sense to use the cabinet for other appliances, e.g., an icebox, refrigerator, or sink.

The actual cabinetwork must be left to the individual converter. Space permits only some vague hints. Construct a box with generous dimensions (Figs. 7-1 and 7-2). There should be at least 2 inches between the edge of the stove and the edge of the moun-

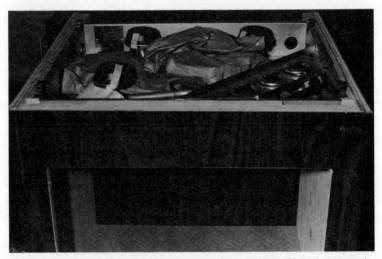

Fig. 7-1. Built-in stoves are designed to drop into cabinets. Note that controls are at right, next to burners. Top-mounted burners require less wiring through the cabinet face. The area below the stove can be used for an ice chest or refrigerator.

Fig. 7-2. This is the underside of a slightly different built-in stove. The fuel tank is next to the single burner and the control valve goes to the front of the cabinet.

ting surface. A pine top, covered with Formica, is the most popular technique. Make the cuts carefully. Vents or portholes have wider edges and some error is tolerable. Most stoves are designed with only a thin mounting edge, so a mistake could mean doing the top over.

Assume that doesn't happen. With the cabinet built, and the mounting hole cut, the complete stove should drop into place and be secured with tabs or mounting flanges. These units are intended for universal application, and the controls are housed in the unit rather than through the cabinet.

(Note for time of purchases. A folding cover for the burners, as shown in Fig. 7-3, is nice to have. It keeps stray objects out of the works, and the folded cover doubles as counter space when cooking isn't taking place.)

BUTANE TANKS

The smaller stoves use bottles of compressed butane that plug into the stove lines. You simply buy a refill every so many hours. For the larger stove, or the larger family, or the giant conversion with a furnace, oven, or butane-powered refrigerator, the demand for fuel will be more than a small refillable bottle can supply.

The answer is a butane tank, permanently installed at the van's lower edge, where the sides roll under, between the front rear wheels (Fig. 7-4).

Fig. 7-3. This tiny built-in two-burner has a cover that folds down to convert the stove top to counter space.

RV and mail-order stores can supply these tanks and the installation kit you'll need. The kit consists of brackets, which go around the tank and extend up to the van floor, and a metal shield, which attaches to the brackets and protects the tank proper from

Fig. 7-4. Chassis-mounted tanks for butane, propane, and LP gas systems are sold in kits that contain a protective shield, pressure regulator, and enough hose for an average installation.

rocks, potholes, etc. (Fig. 7-5).

The lower curve of the van body side must be cut away. Measure the length of the tank and protection plate and find a clear space at the outside edge of the van floor. Which side isn't critical, but it's easier to place the tank on the same side as the stove, so there's less line. Be generous here, too. Allow an extra inch at each end. Make the vertical cuts all the way up to the floor, then connect the two vertical cuts with a horizontal cut. A hacksaw will suffice, but a saber saw is quicker and easier. Hold the mounting bolts and bracket up against the floor and mark where they hit. Drill the holes, install the bolts and nuts, and put the tank and plate in place (Fig. 7-6).

The tank will need a regulator valve, which keeps the output pressure even while the tank goes from high to low, and lines from the valve to stove. Check your local laws for the type of line as they often fall under the influence of building codes. There are no particular problems with the lines, except that they should be curved as gently as possible and should be wrapped in tape, insulation, or similar material where they run through a body panel.

VENTILATION

Ventilation can be a bother. There is a minimum height to be

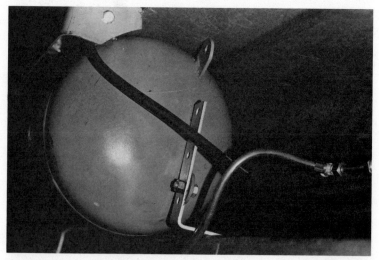

Fig. 7-5. This tank is mounted between the lower body side, at left, and the right-hand frame rail. L-shaped brackets fit into the rail and the tabs on the tank. Routing the hose isn't critical, but always us locally approved material and fittings.

Fig. 7-6. A rock shield protects the pressure regulator and valves. Even a tank tucked away like this decreases ground clearance, so extra care is needed when driving off-road.

Fig. 7-7. Built-in stoves, refrigerators, ovens, furnaces, and other appliances using butane or LP gas require ventilation. Vents are attached with self-tapping screws. Position is vital, so follow manufacturer's directions. (Object on left is a through-the-wall filler for water tank.)

Fig. 7-8. World Industries' galley module contains a stove, sink, water pump, water tank, and ice chest, all in one. It's heavy enough to stay in place on the van floor, light enough to be lifted out for stocking and service.

Fig. 7-9. The World module can be placed nearly anywhere inside the van.

observed, and the law may make you have an outlet—a chimney, in effect—above the stove. Butane appliances also need a lower vent to the outside (Fig. 7-7). Butane is heavier than air. If there is a leak, unventilated gas will sink to the floor and build up until it hits a flame or spark.

All you need is a small vent on the wall above the burners or lines. Mark this point on the inside of the van, drill a hole, and cut a larger hole through the wall. Over that goes the vent, actually a metal plate with louvers. As always, check your RV dealer for the parts.

MODULAR GALLEY

A modular galley is simpler. The one shown in Figs. 7-8 and

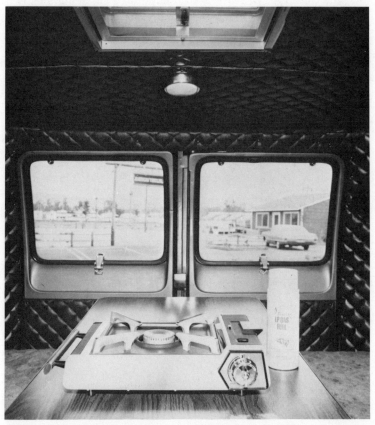

Fig. 7-10. When space and money are limited, and you're willing to serve dinner one course at a time, the truly portable Trav'ler camp stove is ideal.

7-9 is sold under the name "Camp-Kitchen" and comes from World Industries, 1370 Mirasol Street, Los Angeles, CA, 90023. The cabinet is molded fiberglass. Into the cabinet go a two-burner propane stove, a 50-pound icebox, a sink, hand-powered pump, and 10-gallon water tank. It's light enough to be lifted in and out of the van. It's heavy enough to remain in place without being bolted to the floor. It even comes in colors.

What else is there to say? These days one hesitates to name a price on anything, but at this writing the rig sold for less than $360. I won't be surprised if other firms come out with units like this one in the near future. Watch the ads.

PORTABLE STOVE

The third type of stove is the simplest of all, being mostly a refinement on the camping cookers of yesterday. The one shown in Fig. 7-10 is made by Trav'ler and is available at a good RV or camping store. It is a base, with burners, a cover, controls, and a tube, into which the user plugs a smallish butane bottle. It can be stored anywhere and is light and handy to carry around. It can be used on a countertop, floor, picnic table, or the ground. The small stove produces as much cooking heat as the cook can use and with two burners, you have as much convenience as you have with the larger built-in unit. Perhaps this reveals prejudice, but I've watched the construction of the full-dress built-in stove and I've used both the built-in and the small portable. I wouldn't bother with the built-in.

But that's your decision. Anyway you go, it's good to have a van with kitchen facilities.

Chapter 8

Tire Mounts

Vans are supposed to carry things, and the van converter begins with a van for just this reason. Even so, when we modify a van, it is to prepare it to carry what we want. That may not be what the factory expected us to carry, nor will we want some required items in their original locations.

The spare tire is a case in point. Flats are becoming rare, thanks to better tires and roads, but few motorists are willing to dispense with the spare. You may never need one, but it's nice to know it's there.

The makers put the spare in the right rear corner nowadays, usually bolted against the wall. It's okay for commercial use, or when it's covered by a panel in a passenger van, but when you install a custom interior or build in cabinets, etc., the spare has to go somewhere else. One of the interior-kit producers considers this such a mandatory change that an outside mount and tire cover are part of that kit.

Outside mounts almost always go on the right rear door, where they won't use up space that can be used for anything else. The mount itself is a metal framework, roughly triangular, with mounting plates at the corners and a section in the middle that accepts a flat piece that holds the tire in place. The mount isn't complicated, the installation itself is one of the easiest you'll be asked to do, and the mounting kits can be bought from any van or RV store.

Tire mounts come in different models for different makes. The right-hand mounting brackets attach to the upper and lower hinges of the right-hand rear door, while the left-hand leg goes against the inside edge of that door. Different makes and models have different sized doors, so be careful to specify when ordering.

Tools required are a drill and two bits, a hammer and punch, and several hand wrenches. The sizes of each depends upon the sizes of the bolts and nuts in the mount kit. (Most kits are delivered with all needed hardware included.) Check when you buy. If there are no bolts and nuts, a quick look at the holes and locations of the brackets should enable you to get the right pieces from the hardware store.

INSTALLATION

First step is to mark the center of the outside surface of the door's upper hinge. Knock a mark into the surface with the punch,

Fig. 8-1. Drilling holes in the rear-door hinge is the first step.

Fig. 8-2. Bolts for the left leg go through the leg and the door edge, just clearing the door's inner panel.

then drill the proper hole. Get as close to the center as you can.

The mount was designed to fit, but just in case, put it in place and slide the bolt through the upper hole. Position the mount with the lower-right bracket against the surface of the lower hinge. Line up correctly? With the mount vertical and with the left-hand leg even with the edge of the door, the lower right-hand bracket should have its hole in the center of the lower hinge surface (Fig. 8-1). A fraction-of-an-inch error won't matter, but wherever the mounting hole falls, use that hole to mark the place for the lower right-hand bolt. Dimple the lower hinge's outside surface with the punch, remove the mount itself, and drill the hole for the lower bolt.

Put the mount back in place and insert both right-hand bolts. Put on the washers and nuts and snug the bolts down. Don't use the wrenches yet (there's a chance you'll have to juggle the mount around a bit before the job is over).

The left-hand bracket should have its outside edge right at the door's edge (Fig. 8-2). The holes you'll drill must fit between the door edge and the door's inside panel, so be sure the alignment is right.

A good way to be sure the holes are in the correct spot is to use the mounting bracket holes as guides. A pair of locking pliers can be used to hold bracket and door together. Use a bit the same size as the holes in the bracket, to avoid chewing up the sides if the bit hops about, and drill through the door (Fig. 8-3). Take off the pliers, insert bolts, attach washers and nuts, and tighten the bracket down (Fig. 8-4). Because everything lined up, you can tighten the other bolts as well.

Finally, the mounting of the tire. It rests in place on the lower legs of the mount, and there's a short strap that spans the inside of the wheel spider (Fig. 8-5). In the strap is a hole and a long bolt to go through that hole to a captive nut in the mount. The head of this bolt is the same size as the heads of the lug nuts, so the tire can be removed and remounted without extra tools.

For a final touch you can buy tire covers, fiberglass or fabric, in colors that match the van or with slogans.

OTHER IDEAS

The preferred setup today is the continental-type tire cover that

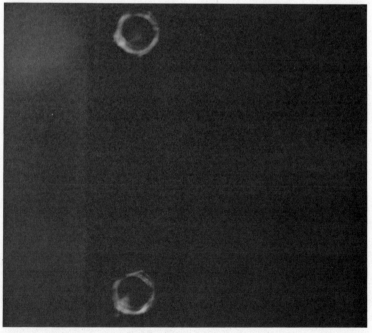

Fig. 8-3. The holes at the door edge must be precisely placed. Use the left leg of the mount as a guide.

Fig. 8-4. Four holes, four bolts, and the framework is attached.

Fig. 8-5. Tire and wheel ride on the strut in the previous picture. The mounting bolt and bracket fasten to the framework, and the nut is the same size as the wheel nuts, so extra tools aren't necessary.

Fig. 8-6. Metal continental tire covers feature a chromed outer retaining ring and can be custom painted.

Fig. 8-7. A novel approach to tire storage is this hassock built into the van's interior decor. The spare is hidden away in the compartment under the cushion.

features a chrome outer ring and a black steel plate that can be custom painted or lettered (Fig. 8-6). These are attractive as well as sturdy and do much to enhance the outer appearance of the van.

Some van owners do not find outside tire mounting and storage appealing. If properly thought out, alternate solutions will enable the owner to store and keep his spare inside the van. It can be hidden by building an inner component (Fig. 8-7) to house the spare and conceal it while performing another useful or decorative function. Another solution (if one has a raised bed compartment in the rear of the van) is to hide the tire under the bed compartment. Whether the tire is to be mounted inside or outside the van is up to the owner's discretion.

Chapter 9

Cabinetry

This is a miscellaneous chapter. Earlier note was made of the impossibility of doing a complete course in cabinetmaking as part of a book on van conversions. True, but at the same time various tips, hints, and trends make themselves so clear that they can't be ignored. This isn't step-by-step stuff, more like a couple of starting points, some pictures of finished work, several shots of work in progress, and a few details.

The most important point is that the van converter who wishes to do really individual projects must do some carpentry. There's no way out. You can buy a module stove or a sink or a combination and accept someone else's idea of what should go where. You can do without. Or you can buy the actual component, build a stand or cabinet, and place it where you want.

The same principle works with some types of interior changes, i.e., a raised floor with storage compartment or panels to separate one part of the van from another. It seems like most converted cruiser vans have these items, but nobody sells the completed pieces. Why not? Because they're simple to make.

BOLSTERS

We'll start with the raised rear platform. People in the trade call them *bolsters*. This doesn't go with what the dictionary says, but because it's a common term, we'll use it.

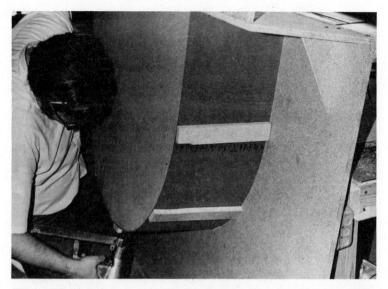

Fig. 9-1. The bolster floor is stapled to the inside, curved section. Note the pine strips that serve as legs for the top surface and as reinforcements for the curved wall.

A bolster is a large box, usually wall-to-wall, and extended from the rear-floor edge to the front of the fender wells. Most bolsters have small hatches in the rear vertical panel for storage of the spare tire, tools, valuables, etc. Some bolsters are made with a semicircle cutout in the front, so the raised floor serves as a couch. Some are covered with foam beneath carpet of vinyl to serve as couch and bed.

Size, shape, usage, and so forth are entirely up to the builder. A bolster is cheaper than a factory-made bed or couch. It can have hatches for storage, or be used to hide a water tank, or whatever. There is no point, then, in giving dimensions or designs.

The starting point for a bolster is 3/8-inch particle board. It comes in large sheets, it's strong enough for this purpose, and it cuts and shapes more easily than plywood. To make a bolster, decide how wide it will be, or how wide the van is, and how long. Measure and cut a rectangle. Side, front, and rear wall measurements follow (that is, as wide or long as the top, and as high as you want the floor). Usually the floor will be just high enough to clear the fender well, and usually the bolster top will rest on the well, so *that* dimension is taken care of.

Particle board is strong, but it isn't thick. Rather than join one panel to the other, use pine board, 1 × 1 inch or close to that, as

81

a joiner (Fig. 9-1). Fasten one wall to the pine with wood screws, put the wall in proper position with the top, drill, and attach the top to the board.

You are building a box, with top, four sides, and no floor. When the sides are assembled, test for fit. The bolster should be as wide as the floor space, so you'll have to tip it on its side, boost it through the rear door, and let it slip into position. You're aiming for a press fit, so let's hope it does. As with every other project in this book, planning and careful measurement are vital, and it won't hurt if you check the fit on the top by setting it on the floor before you attach the sides.

A bolster with a cut-out center section is more involved (Fig. 9-2). First, decide how large the semicircular notch should be. Then take a string of the desired radius, tie a pencil to one end, and fasten the other end in the exact center of the top panel. Scribe a half circle, and cut along the line with a saber saw or keyhole saw.

Save the removed section. It will be the floor. Measure the half circumference you just cut. Buy some thin beaver board or hard cardboard, 1/8 inch thick. It must be thin because it will curve along the cutout and will be the inset section of the bolster's front edge. To force this panel to hold its curve, you need some pine board, 1 × 2 inch, as long as the bolster is high. Five or six of these props will do it. Place them evenly around the edge and attach them to

Fig. 9-2. A completed, unupholstered bolster with cutout. The rear corners are trimmed slightly to clear the panels next to the rear door.

Fig. 9-3. With construction completed, the bolster is given a foam pad. Shag carpet is glued and tacked over the foam. Note the reinforcements behind the beaver board-faced cutout.

the top panel. The two side front panels should be fastened to the top and the curved panel forced into place (Fig. 9-3). (This is another time when two people do the best work.) Fasten one end of the curved panel to the front side panel and work around the semicircle. If you have a power or automatic staple gun, this is the time to use it. If not, small tacks will work. The curved panel won't be under stress, so the time and bother of using wood screws isn't justified.

Upholstering the bolster is almost exactly like upholstering the van floor. You can use carpet or vinyl with foam pad or without. Trim the panels to fit, spray on glue, and press the covering into place. There are no compound curves here.

A note for the cautious. To the outsider the bolster doesn't look very strong. Lots of unsupported surface, and people will be sitting on it. Don't worry, the pros say. Particle board will hold up. And so it seems. Just in case, though, some of the builders install brackets at the front and rear walls to support the top (Fig. 9-4). Scraps will work, they say, and you can simply screw the bracket into place. (Nobody uses legs, although they'd be easy to make.) I reckon the builders must be correct, and the construction shown is sufficient.

A storage door is optional (Fig. 9-5). All it takes is an oval cut in the rear wall, with a saber saw, any size you please. Hinges from

Fig. 9-4. For extra bracing, a scrap of particle board is inserted between the bolster top and rear wall.

the hardware store and a pull handle complete the job. Fabric or rug can be glued over the door.

CABINETS

Cabinets are much more involved. The task is to build a container for the icebox, sink, stove, or perhaps all three at once.

One more time—planning. The dimensions of the appliance being fitted are obviously vital and available. Retail stores and mail-order firms carefully list the width, depth, height, weight, etc., for the various models. The builders of the equipment realize their products will be going into a variety of places, and they provide mounting flanges. The lip of the sink, for example, or of the edge of the icebox just inside the door, are designed to align with the opening of the cabinet.

The homebuilder needs to know how big the various items are. That taken care of, you next must know the space available in the van: the distance from the back of the driver's seat to the fender well, or whatever. With both sets of dimensions, you can calculate whether the icebox, sink, and oven you have in mind can be fitted into a cabinet that will fit in the van.

The pros use two methods. One is to make a frame from strips of pine or other softwood, into which the appliances are fitted and over which go panels. The latter method requires a hardwood veneer or softwood covered with vinyl. Another approach is to use particle board for the frame, with openings cut for the appliances and 1 × 2-inch pine strips around the openings, to attach the stove or icebox.

The pine frame method is neater and quicker *if you have the skill*. To understand the emphasis, look at the pictures (Figs. 9-6 and 9-7). Nice work, but the maker must be very good at measur-

Fig. 9-5. The bolster for this van has a cargo hatch cut into the rear wall for stowing a spare tire and for access to a water tank mounted beneath the bolster floor. (The panel cut from the wall can be hinged and used as a door.)

Fig 9-6. A front frame of precisely fitted pine, stapled together. The beginning cabinetmaker may find this difficult.

ing all those pieces, at having all right angles just so, and having access to a commercial-type staple gun.

The particle board panel allows for some slight error. Mark the openings on the panel, cut them out, and fasten pine strips to

Fig. 9-7. Good work pays off. The built-in icebox fits perfectly into the opening. Side spaces will be used as storage cabinets. Formica will cover the particle board top.

Fig. 9-8. One method for building cabinets. Particle board is used for the outline, backed with a pine where extra strength is needed.

the edges. One piece slightly off center won't throw the entire job out of whack (Fig. 9-8).

Either way, the top and side panels can be particle board, joined with pine strips (Fig. 9-9). Covering varies with taste. Lumber yards

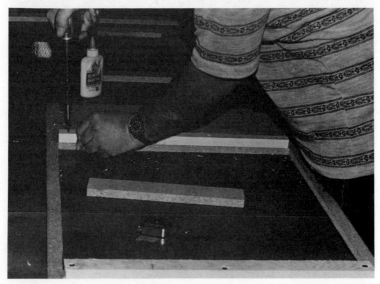

Fig. 9-9. Reinforcing strips are fastened with wood screws. Fit should be close, but doesn't have to be perfect.

have thin, fancy hardwood veneers in any exotic wood you could want (Fig. 9-10). Or cover with vinyl to match the interior walls. The top can be Formica, also easily found in various colors or patterns. A good do-it-yourself supply store will have aluminum strips for the edges, as well as handles and hinges for the doors.

Fig. 9-10. Completed frame is laid over hardwood veneer, which is cut and glued onto the frame.

Fig. 9-11. Shaping a divider to exactly conform to the curves of wall and headliner is tough. Begin with a freehand curve, then cut and file slight corrections until it's flush.

ROOM DIVIDERS

Third comes room dividers, the panels that fasten to the van wall and ceiling and separate the rear from the center or the living room from the driving compartment. They are popular in cruising vans. They are also strictly for looks as no function is served that wouldn't be served just as well by a curtain.

Looks are important. The dividers are also particle board. The different part here is calculating the curve of the ceiling. No two vans are alike, especially if the ceiling panels are part of a kit installed by the owner.

Take a large piece of poster board, like the stuff the kids use for art in school. Look at the curve from the wall and ceiling joint to where you want the divider to end. Freehand that curve on the poster board. Cut along the line, hold it up against the ceiling, see where it doesn't touch, trim, try again, and so on. See Fig. 9-11. Measure the height of the walls and decide how far in you wish the dividers to protrude. Transfer these measurements and the ceiling pattern to the particle board and cut to fit.

Each ceiling joint curve should be done for itself. The left side and right side may not be exactly symmetrical. The inner curves, though, should be marked with the same pattern. It works best if you put the two panels together and cut these two inner curves at the same time (Fig. 9-11). They must be exactly alike or the dividers will look like trash.

With the dividers cut out, hold them in place and see if they fit properly. Judging from the struggles the top custom shops go through with dividers, they won't fit right. Trim off the high spots with a rough file until there's no daylight showing along the joint of interior wall and ceiling.

The actual shape doesn't matter. The dividers shown are on onion dome, most unusual (Fig. 9-12). Generally, a simple curve is all that's tackled. The onion dome was a new concept, and it took some persuasion by the carpenter before the shop owner would let him try it.

Attaching the divider to the wall and ceiling is awkward. There's no good, thick, concealed place to do it. A pine block fastened to the wall panel and the divider panel is best, but you'll have to slit the upholstery panels and stuff the block in, install the screws, and glue the material back in place. At the center of the ceiling, a screw through the divider tip into the panel will work.

The dividers must be covered before they're finally fastened into place. Vinyl to match the interior is the obvious material. Cut the fabric to match the divider and sew the two edges together (Fig.

Fig. 9-12. Dividers can be works of art. Elaborate series of cuts will work best if the two halves are cut at the same time while clamped together.

Fig. 9-13. When the fit is perfect, the dividers are covered with fabric. The exact outline is traced on vinyl, then the outside seam is sewn together and the cover glued over the board.

9-13). This is tricky, obviously. Spray glue on the divider and tug the covers into position. The edges next to the wall can be stapled in place and should be carefully trimmed after that.

Now for my little "editorial" note: the more I review the notes

Fig. 9-14. The completed job—a bolster with dividers.

and pictures, the more I recall how much time and sweat professional installers invest in these dividers. Because they're just for looks, I wouldn't do them. But then, you needn't do any of this carpentry work. It looks fine (Fig. 9-14), but there are ways around building your own cabinets.

Chapter 10

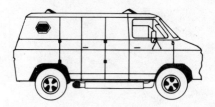

Plumbing

Three pieces of equipment are grouped together in this chapter because the three are integral. The sink, the tank, and the pump are a water-supply system, and the van without all three pieces might as well not have any.

The first consideration might be if the van needs water. Water systems take space. If water is needed only for drinking, you'll do better to buy a big insulated jug and figure some way to store it. People don't need to drink more than a few gallons over the week-end, and in most locations, portable water isn't hard to find.

Water systems are used mostly for washing dishes and hands, which is why you also have sinks. Rough-it campers won't need the system, but two people on tour, cooking three meals a day and using genuine plates and silver, will find the system invaluable.

WATER TANKS

Water tanks come in a good selection of sizes, from 20 gallons—as big as you'll be able to pack into a van—down to 5 gallons. Any van shop seriously doing business will be able to supply whatever size you need, and you can also check the camping stores and army-surplus places. A water tank is just a large plastic box. (Before snapping up a bargain, though, be mighty sure the tank hasn't been used for holding other fluids. Chemicals are nearly impossible to clean out of a plastic tank.)

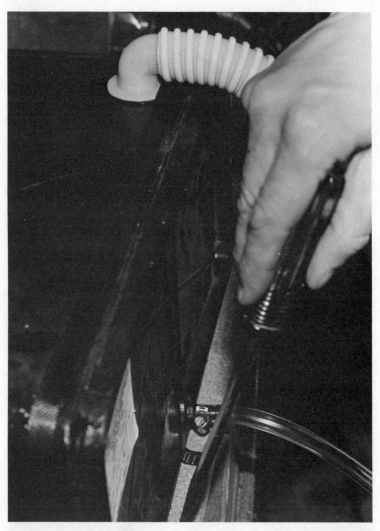

Fig. 10-1. The filler pipe (top) is glued into position. The outlet pipe (clear line, bottom center) fastens with a hose clamp to a metal outlet fitting.

Larger tanks, say 12 gallons and up, work best mounted under the van floor, generally between the body sides and the frame rails. Tanks designed for vans are long and narrow and will fit into this space. The closer to the sink the better, so when you're planning the galley, try to place the sink above this space in the chassis. It's not hard, by the way, as the clear space above and below almost always falls between the rear wheels and the side doors.

Underfloor tanks are sold with mounting brackets, usually a steel plate slightly larger than the tank and steel frames to slip over the front and rear. There are holes through these frames and long bolts pass through them and the floor.

Before fitting the tank, attend to the various inlets and outlets. There should be a filler pipe, an outlet for the pump, a drain, and an air vent to avoid air locks and bubbles.

The vent should come from the top of the tank. (The stores selling tanks are also able to provide the fittings and hoses.) Drill the hole, use the glue from the same store, and let it dry. If the tank is inside the van, under cover, then coiling the hose once or twice and taping it to the top of the tank is all you'll need to do. If the tank goes under the floor, you'll need some space, such as two or three slats of 1-inch pine, to separate the tank top and floor bottom. Again, just coil the hose and fasten it down.

The filler pipe should also go into the tank top. Where it points depends on where you put the inlet fitting. The installation pictured in Fig. 10-1 has the intake under the sink. You can also put an intake, of a slightly different type, through the side of the van. A high intake can be routed behind the interior wall and through the floor, but it's easier—assuming an underfloor tank—to locate the fitting just above the inlet pipe, so you only need to go through one metal wall.

Fig. 10-2. This 10-gallon tank is mounted on a sheet of particle board bolted to the van floor. Hidden beneath a bolster, it is held in place with vinyl straps stapled to the floor.

Keep the inlet hose as short as possible. Tape or pad it where it comes close to an edge or hard surface and be careful not to kink it.

The outlet should come out of the side of the tank, right at the bottom edge. No location problems here, assuming the sink is

Fig. 10-3. Pine framework for a cabinet that will hold a sink and water pump. It is attached to the left-hand interior wall and the side of a divider. Hoses route through gaps designed into the panels.

Fig. 10-4. The cabinet top has been sized and the holes cut for the sink and pump inlet. Bracket at left will hold the filler pipe inlet.

nearby. The outlet hose is usually hidden by interior panels or cabinetwork. Once more, plastic hose and fittings will do fine, because water isn't particularly corrosive and there's no pressure to speak of.

Drains are sometimes considered an option, but not by me. Water does go stale, and the van may not be used for camping every day. It's easier to let the old run out than to have to flush it out.

For an underfloor tank, a small fitting in the lowest corner will suffice. Hunker down, pull the plug, and stand clear. If the tank is inside the van, especially if it's underneath a bolster or tucked into the back of the cabinet, the drain is more of a problem (Fig. 10-2). The only good way to solve it is to fit a small hose to a fitting on the lowest corner, run said hose through the floor and across the van to the lower edge of the body, fasten it to the body with a C-clamp, and pop a valve onto the end.

The only risk is that a rock or something will hit the hose and pull it loose, letting all the water escape. This is rare in real life, while crawling into the cabinet to turn a protected valve is a hardship you'd need to do after every trip.

But we are ahead of ourselves. Everything should be measured and located. You should know where the various hoses are going. The proper holes should be cut, and the fittings should be fitted to the tank.

To install the tank, fit the frames and hold the tank up against the floor—once more, with the aid of a friend. Mark where the bolts touch, drill holes, and reassemble the tank and frames with the protection plate also gripped by the frames. This isn't critical, but it's easier to drop the bolts down through the floor and guide them into the frame holes, then raise the assembly against the floor and fasten the nuts.

SINKS

The tank is in place. When we come to the sink, we come to

Fig. 10-5. The nearly completed cabinet shows the mounting hole for the sink and the position of the filler pipe bracket. When the door is added, the bracket, caps, and hose will be out of sight.

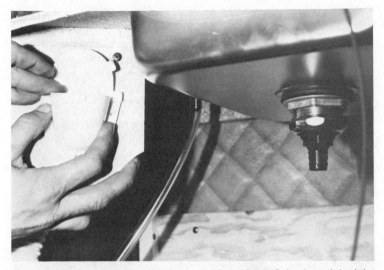

Fig. 10-6. The sink has been dropped into place. Drain fitting is at right. Inlet fitting is being installed at left.

more cabinetwork. There are complete kitchen units on the market (see Chapter 7), but most of the makers of sinks produce just sinks and fittings.

The installation pictures (Figs. 10-3 through 10-6) show a typical

Fig. 10-7. The pump drops through the hole and fastens with wood screws to the counter top.

and tidy cabinet for a sink. All it takes is a front with a door and a solid countertop, perhaps with a Formica covering.

Sinks come in various shapes—oval, square, and round. With the countertop completed, place the sink, upside down, where you want it to be. Trace around the edge, lift the sink off, and cut around the traced line with a saber saw. The sink can be flipped over and dropped into place.

Built-in sinks are sold with metal tabs welded to the underside.

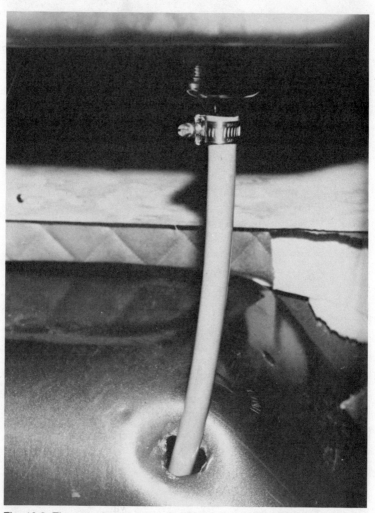

Fig. 10-8. There are better ways to build a drain than to route a plastic hose from the drain fitting through a hole punched in the fender well.

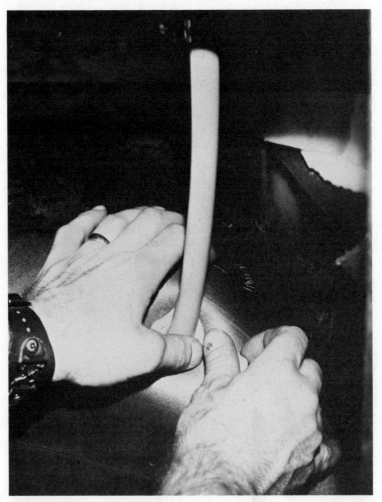

Fig. 10-9. Sealer will prevent chafing of the drain hose and seal out spray, cold air, and noise.

The tabs can be bent over and pressed against the underside of the cabinet. The tabs have holes. Drill guide holes into the wood and fasten the sink to the top with wood screws.

PUMP, HOSES, AND DRAIN

The pump in Fig. 10-7 is a manual model, meaning it has a handle that you shove back and forth to deliver water. There are electric pumps on the market, but they seldom appear in vans converted by owners as they cost more, use electricity, and do nothing a manual pump won't do.

With sink in place, position the pump at a convenient edge. Mark the edges—close enough is good enough—and in the center of the markings cut a round hole big enough for the tube at the base of the pump to go through. Put the pump in place, with the tube down the hole, and drill guide holes through the mounting holes in the pump base. Fasten with wood screws, and the pump is installed.

The hoses for the various fittings can be light plastic because there are no problems with weight, pressure, or temperature. With the hardware installed, simply run the hoses from one fitting to the other and tighten with hose clamps (Fig. 10-8).

We still need a drain. I blush for the one shown (Fig. 10-8). The principle is fine—a plastic hose attaches to the sink outlet. But this shop runs its drains through the van's fender well and out onto the ground, which is not a neighborly thing to do. If you'd rather vans had a good name, leave undersink space for a 5-gallon jerry can, run the drain hose into that, and dump the can in a socially approved location (Fig. 10-9).

Chapter 11

Beds

Conversion of a van into a truly mobile home requires a place to sleep. How many people can be accommodated and the degree of comfort provided depend upon the builder's intentions. One could, if desired, just plop the entire family down on the floor and let that be enough.

But for most builders, a place to sleep means a bed with a mattress and a surface raised off the floor by a foot or so. Much planning is needed here, both before you pick the type and size bed needed, and before you install it.

First things first. Sleeping room for two adults will require a lot of space, say 4 × 6 feet. Remove that from the interior floor space of a long van or even a Dodge Maxi, and you haven't much room remaining. We'll assume, therefore, that the bed must either stow away or convert into something else during the day. A good van conversion is like a boat in this respect, with every piece of equipment designed to serve at least two purposes while taking up as little room as possible.

We are in luck. There are firms designing and building convertible beds for vans and other recreational vehicles. We don't need to build our own, but need only make them fit our plans and floor space.

We are also in for a bit of a search. We've already noted that vans for living need beds. We know there are lots of vans being converted, and that there are firms catering to this market.

Odd, then, that none of the mail-order firms and few of the RV shops stock beds. The problem seems to be one of bulk. Beds are big and heavy. They are hard to store and expensive to ship. Further, they are expensive. It's likely mail-order houses don't like to cram their warehouses full of items that take up space, tie up capital, and move slowly.

Perhaps because of this the manufacturers are willing to deal directly with the customer. The major firms do most of their business with the wholesale converters, but they are willing to sell one unit to one person. Because there are no showrooms, you may not be able to see what you're ordering until it's on your front step. Take your time. The sellers will provide brochures, dimensions, weights, fabric choices, etc. Study the data and proceed with deliberation. (At the end of this chapter is a list with the names and addresses of bed suppliers.)

The types, sizes, and methods of installation of the various van beds vary, as you'd guess. One set of instructions won't do it. Instead, we'll look at several beds to see what they will do and how much work is involved.

UNILOUNGE

Any van bed should convert into something else or stow away. The *UniLounge* does the former and does it well. By day the UniLounge is a pair of two-person bench seats. They may be a bit small for adults, but kids fit fine, and this bed/seat system is a good one for a van that transports children. You can tuck the units up next to a window and fit them with seatbelts.

The UniLounge comes in two units. Each has two halves and three positions. For traveling, both units are upright, with seat back and seat cushion set so the passenger faces forward. As an alternative, the forward unit can be swung completely through its arc of travel. The cushion becomes the seat and vice versa, and the forward unit now faces to the rear. There is space between the cushions, and you can install a small table between the seats. Presto, the dining room!

At night, both units can be released from their upright positions. The two halves slide toward each other and seat backs completely recline. The four upholstered sections become one long mattress, with the two halves just pressing against each other. And you have a double bed large enough for growing children or an adult of no more than average size.

The UniLounge itself arrives nearly complete. All the buyer

must do is bolt on the covers for the armrests and attach a few minor fittings.

Nor is the actual mounting of the units that difficult. Below the cushions are legs of steel tubing with mounting flanges attached to them (Fig. 11-1). The flanges have holes. All you need to do is bolt these flanges to the floor.

Where do you do that? This is the tricky part. First you must figure out where in the van the units should or will fit. The logical place is up against the left wall, just aft of the driver's seat, so the seat/bed is out of the way and can be close to a window. Trouble is, the units may not fit there. This depends on the brand of van and length of the wheelbase. The shorter of the short vans don't have enough space between the seat and the wheel well (Fig. 11-2). Go or no-go can even depend on how far back the driver likes his seat to be.

The first thing to do is get the measurements of the UniLounge and try them against the dimensions of your van. You need length, width, and the height of the cushion from the floor. The mounting legs are inboard of the cushions, so if the bed itself is high enough to be above the wheel well, not having enough clear floor space won't matter.

If the UniLounge won't fit against the wall, experiment (Figs. 11-3 and 11-4). How far from the wall—and the wheel—must it be? Will this block your aisle? Are seats and a bed for the kids worth blocking the aisle? (I watched one good team of installers struggle

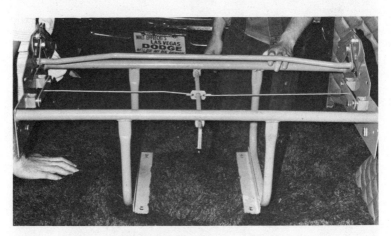

Fig. 11-1. Frame for a UniLounge. The legs and mounting holes are close to center, so there's usually no trouble finding a place to drill, but fitting two units into a short van can be difficult.

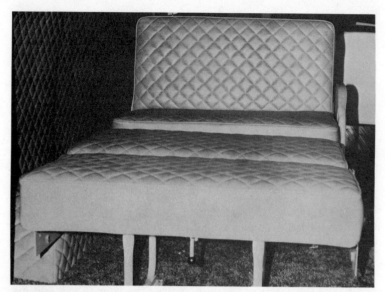

Fig. 11-2. In this installation the side panel didn't clear the fender well and the bed runs from driver's seat to rear door.

for a full day trying to fit too large a bed into a short van. It couldn't be done in any way that made it worth doing. Check this before you buy.)

Fig. 11-3. In a Maxiwagon, the UniLounge can be used for daytime seats.

Fig. 11-4. The UniLounge opened to a bed. Note that all four sections are flat, and that the two pieces have been placed so they just meet each other.

Enough pessimism. Let's assume the bed itself will fit. The next step is to accurately locate the mounting bolt holes in the floor—and let me warn once again that if it's possible, do this sort of chore before installing the interior panels and rug.

You can, if you wish, place the units in the van, position both so they align with each other, then check the floor to be sure you can drill holes below the legs. That'll work fairly well.

The pros have a better way, although it takes extra time and a few dollars. Buy some sheets of cheap plywood, panelboard, or whatever. It merely has to be larger than the bed units, thin, and flat.

Flop the boards down on a large vacant space, like the garage floor. Put the units in the middle of the panels. Push both into the full-recline position and ease them up against each other. Make sure they're exactly aligned. Mark where the mounting holes will be. Trace a rough outline of the edges of the beds on the board. Remove beds, drill holes, and cut along the outline.

You now have a template for the UniLounge. Position the template in the van, just where you want the beds to be. When you have the exact spot, take a punch and mark the holes on the van floor. Spend a few minutes popping in and beneath the van, so you don't drill into the tank or the wires, and drill the holes. Leave the template in position, naturally, so when the eight holes are drilled to pattern, the actual installation will be a breeze.

THE TEN-SECOND BED

The *Ten-Second Bed* is relatively new on the market, and it's designed more for the motorcycle or hauling-van folks than for van campers. It's a full double bed that folds up against the wall, like the Murphy beds from the slapstick movies.

The maker is *Hydra Products Co.* The bed itself is more of a kit for a bed frame than a complete unit (Fig. 11-5). You buy the pieces for the frame and all related hardware from Hydra. You also need two sheets of 3/8-inch plywood, 24 × 71 inches, and two 3 × 24 × 72-inch foam pads (Fig. 11-6). The buyer can find the finished units in a camping supply house or may buy the foam and the fabric and cover the former with the latter.

The principle of this installation is tricky, which means I had to watch one work before I could understand how it worked. The pictures here are not quite accurate. The Hydra bed comes in two models: one for vans, the other for pickup trucks. The only installation in progress that I could find at press time was in a truck, so

Fig. 11-5. A foldaway bed kit contains the metal framework. You make the wood panels. Note the mounting hinges at right. To fold, the left half of the frame slides into the right half.

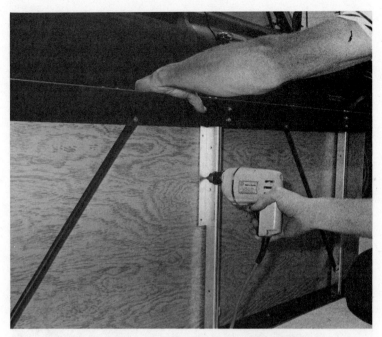

Fig. 11-6. The wood panels attach to the frame with wood screws.

that's what you see. (Not to worry. The only difference in the models is the brackets that attach the inside edge of the frame to the wall.)

The brackets are also hinges. The frame thus goes parallel to the wall, in the raised position, or at right angles to it. There are folding legs attached to the frame, so the entire bed extends only 8 inches from the wall (and into the van's living area) when the bed is folded (Fig. 11-7). The legs eliminate any need for cantileverage or side supports.

The frame is actually two frames, one slightly shorter than the other, and so designed that the outside frame slides into the inside frame. The plywood panels are mattress supports that for the outside frame are firmly attached to the metal pieces, brackets, etc. The inside support attaches only at the inside edge, and its outer edge rides over the inner edge of the outside panel when the frames are compressed (Figs. 11-8 through 11-10). The mattress can be separate, although the makers recommend that the covers be attached at the top. This keeps the two pads in place, while letting them fold for storage.

The basic installation should be planned before the interior is done. The converter should know exactly where the bed will be, although finding space for mounting holes on the wall is less of a problem than on the floor.

The frames can be assembled outside the van for working ease. Nothing to this, as the pieces are self-explanatory. Then the assembly can be loaded into the van.

Mounting height for the hinges and brackets isn't vital. The length of this bed surely means it will be above the left fender well, so be careful to have the brackets high enough.

The brackets bolt to the wall ribs (another one of the those jobs best done by two people). Put the hinges on the frame, hold the frame against the wall, be very sure the frame is level, and fasten. Then trim the legs so the bed is level with the floor.

The last major attachment is a strap to keep the bed in an upright position. Fold the bed and mark where the top edge hits the wall. Six or so inches above that, drill a small hole. The bed comes with a strap, bracket, cinch, and clawlike thing that snags

Fig. 11-7. Stowed, the bed takes up only eight inches of space along one wall. (The installation shown is in a camper-equipped pickup truck, but van installation is virtually the same.

Fig. 11-8. With frame unfolded and half the mattress left against the wall, the unit becomes a couch.

the bed side. Use a self-tapping screw to fasten bracket to wall—right to the panel itself. There isn't much momentum or weight to handle. Slip the hook over the bed frame, pull on the strap, cinch it, and the bed is secure against the wall. It only takes 8 inches, so this bed is especially suited to vans that haul motorcycles or great piles of outdoor camping gear.

The bed can also be dropped to the horizontal, but let recessed. One mattress pad can be propped against the wall and the other plopped flat to make a sofa. Not too comfortable, to be truthful, but it can be done. In summary, this unit is a good one for some purposes, but it isn't suited for mobile-home conversions.

GAUCHO BED

There are van beds suited to mobile-home living. In the trade, the name is *gaucho bed*, for reasons unknown. No matter. The gaucho bed is a truly convertible couch. It looks and feels just like the couch in your living room, but the seat portion comes out and the back portion falls flat and you have a double bed (Fig. 11-11).

There are several firms making gauchos. The ones shown here are by *Kustom-Fit*, a major supplier to the professional conversion firms that also sell retail.

The good beds have been carefully designed so the seat and back both lie completely flat and close together. There are brands which haven't done this well, and you get a shallow "V." I dare not list the inferior brands, so I'll urge you to find an example of the unit you want to buy and inspect its sleepworthiness before you send the check.

The next problem is space. There are two sizes of gauchos. The large ones are long enough for two adults of average height. (Length varies, naturally, with brand.) The long jobs must go against the van's let wall. The shorter gauchos are set crossways

Fig. 11-9. The strap to hold the frame against the wall uses a hook and cinch. The wallboard panel is strong enough to support the weight of the bed.

Fig. 11-10. Unfolded and extended, with mattress in place, the Ten-Second Bed is complete.

Fig. 11-11. A gaucho bed can be just like home. This is a longer model designed to sit sideways in the van.

Fig. 11-12. The cushions are critical. This gaucho converts by sliding the seat section out. The backrest is wood. The cushions fit into position between the seat section and the wall.

in the van like a regular car seat. The short units can go up against the rear door or even in the middle of the van, depending upon what else the builder plans to install. The trouble with this is that the bed may not be long enough for you. Get the dimensions first (Fig. 11-12).

After all that planning, the installation is almost too simple to describe. It's a repeat of the work with the UniLounge: place the unit inside the bare van and make sure it has adequate clearance in all positions. The gaucho bolts to the floor via flanges in the bottom of the legs. When the bed is positioned, check to be sure none of the mounting holes are impractical. Mark, drill, and bolt the bed out after drilling and fit the rug before bolting down the bed. It depends on how good you are at fitting the rug around the legs, or whether you prefer the rug to be squashed.

The gaucho is the most comfortable of the three types. It also weighs the most, costs the most, and takes up the most room.

The following are the complete addresses of companies supplying the Ten-Second, UniLounge, and Gaucho beds:

Ten-Second Bed
Hydra Products, Inc.
1320 West Santa Ana Street
Anaheim, CA 92802

UniLounge and Gaucho
Kustom-Fit
14108 South Towne Avenue
Los Angeles, CA 90061

Chapter 12

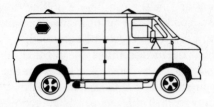

Refrigerators and Iceboxes

Generation gap? There are those of us old enough to remember when every kitchen had an icebox, an insulated box that kept food and ice. This was replaced by a refrigerator, with gas or electricity doing the cooling. Some people, though, still say "icebox" when they mean "refrigerator."

COMPARISON

Better get this straight. Vans can be equipped with iceboxes—insulated boxes that hold food and ice—and with refrigerators—insulated food boxes with equipment to cool themselves. Each serves the same purpose, but beyond that, iceboxes and refrigerators go in different directions.

An icebox holds ice and food, so it follows that the interior space available for food is less than the outside dimensions would indicate. Careful preparation, i.e., the use of dry or canned food wherever practical, will allow weekend camping via the icebox. On the road, plan to restock the larder every day, as you'll have room for little else besides milk, eggs, and meat. Also, keep an eye peeled for places to buy ice. An icebox worth having will hold 25 pounds of ice, but will melt in two or three days, even if you keep the door shut as much as you can.

On the good side, an icebox is cheap: $40 or so for a box with a capacity of 4 cubic feet. A refrigerator of the same exterior size retails for nearly 10 times that. The icebox is also much easier to install, as we'll see.

The advantages of a refrigerator come down mostly to the simple fact that they hold more food. Nearly all the interior is usable stowage space. You can have a freezer and even an ice tray (Fig. 12-1).

Against that is cost and complexity. You know about cost. The complexity comes from having to have an outside source of power for the compressor and blower motor. There are some well-known names—*Mobilaire, Trav'ler, Norcold, Dometic*—and they've all done good work adapting to the demands of motor homes and vans. The better brands now offer combinations of power. The refrigerator can be run off the car's electrical system (12 V) or can be switched over to house current (115 V) if the campsite is so equipped. Other models use the car's battery or LP gas, supplied by a small bottle mounted near the unit or a larger tank set below the van floor. The latest thing is a three-way system with 12 V, 115 V, or LP gas and a three-way switch (Fig. 12-2).

The choices are as varied when it comes to size. There are giant refrigerators, easily adequate for a nonmobile home, but too big—4 feet high by 2 feet wide—to be practical for a van. At the other end of the scale are refrigerators 2 feet high and less than 18 inches wide. For the cost of a refrigerator, so to speak, you get the capacity of an icebox. But if money isn't a hurdle, and if size is compatible

Fig. 12-1. All the interior space of this refrigerator can be used for food, and it even has a freezer with an ice cube tray.

Fig. 12-2. Control switch for a three-way refrigerator that can be powered by butane, the van's 12V system, or 110V household current. (The butane inlet is not connected because this installation will use only electrical power.)

with the other equipment carried, the small jobs are the answer.

The best sources for iceboxes and refrigerators are the mail-order firms. Their catalogs list many brands, types, and sizes, each with dimensions. Both types come as freestanding units, finished outsides and all, or as units that slip into cabinets that the buyer must build (Figs. 12-3 through 12-5).

On that subject there's not much to be said here. This book cannot serve as an introduction to cabinetry. I will have to assume that you will either be able to make your own cabinet, or have it made, or that you will buy an icebox or refrigerator that doesn't need a cabinet.

Built-in iceboxes and refrigerators come with wide lips around the front edges. If the cutout is 19×25 inches, the edges will measure 21×27 inches. The overlap butts against the face of the cabinet; the installer drills holes in the edge, and then mounts the icebox with wood screws. That's all the actual installation amounts to.

An icebox needs a drain hose. The bottom of the box is shaped into a shallow dish with a hole and tube at the lowest point. As the ice melts, the water drips to the floor and out the drain hole. Prepare for this. Drill a hole through the van floor below the drain tube, slip a plastic hose over the tube, and route it through the floor. The

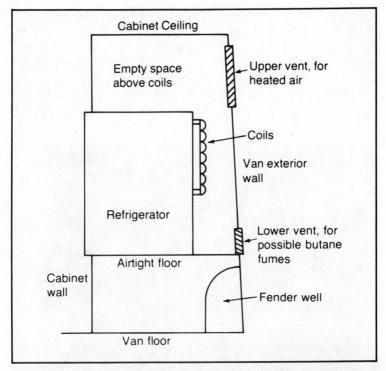

Cabinet Ceiling

Empty space
above coils

Upper vent, for
heated air

Coils

Van exterior
wall

Refrigerator

Lower vent, for
possible butane
fumes

Airtight floor

Cabinet
wall

Fender well

Van floor

Fig. 12-3. A refrigerator should be mounted with generous space between the condenser and cabinet. Note the upper vent for hot air exhaust and the lower vent for butane spillage.

flow of water will be so slight, not even your neighbors will know.

INSTALLATION OF A REFRIGERATOR

The installation of a refrigerator is more difficult. The remarks about cabinetwork in Chapter 9 apply here. The principles are the same.

Allow for more depth than the dimensions of the machine when you build the cabinet. Refrigeration actually is the extraction of heat from inside the box. The heat is transferred outside, to the coils at the rear of the unit, and then to the air. The more air and the better the circulation of the air, the better the unit cools. The minimum is 4 inches clear space between the coils and the van wall. There should be at least 2 inches clear space above the coils.

If the refrigerator uses butane, it needs two vents to the outside. One is for fumes and hot air and should go in the van wall above the top of the coils. The other should have its bottom edge the same height as the bottom of the unit, and there must be a solid, virtually airtight floor below the refrigerator. Butane is heavier than air. If there are any leaks, the gas will sink to the floor. With the vent, it escapes to the outside. Without ventilation butane can build up inside and be ignited by a spark. You don't want that.

Electricity is less bother. Once again, plan for this job before you start the interior. The 12 V system needs a ground wire that

Fig. 12-4. Installing an icebox or refrigerator is not difficult. Building the cabinet, however, can be. This cabinet is of particle board faced with veneer and backed with pine around the opening. Note that the interior walls behind the refrigerator have been cut away for extra space and ventilation.

Fig. 12-5. Completed installation. The unit slides into the opening and is fastened with wood screws.

can go to the metal floor panel and a hot wire from the accessory pole on the ignition switch. This provides power when the engine is running and allows refrigerator operation when parked. Right, when parked. Assuming the unit is cold at journey's end, keeping

Fig. 12-6. This refrigerator cabinet is between a pair of dividers. The installers notched the lower inside edge of the divider so the owner can reach behind it to use the switch.

it cold draws only an amp or so on a continuous basis. Opening the door naturally creates more of a demand on the battery, so it's best to have supper and then drive for awhile, or to remember to shut off the refrigerator when parked. Learning how long the refrigerator can be operated without draining the battery takes practice—and caution.

House current requires no more than plugging the cord (supplied with a refrigerator wired for 115 V) into the appropriate receptacle. You can use a long cord from the compressor or fit the van with a through-the-wall adapter, with the female half of the socket on the inside and the male half on the outside. Again, refer to the mail-order houses or check with local stores dealing in van and camping equipment.

In case of the three-way system, as shown in Fig. 12-6, allow for access to the controls. Manufacturers all seem to put them in the rear, back there with the machinery, and reaching the switch can be a problem.

Chapter 13

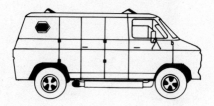

Door Extenders

This project is quite optional. It involves a simple part, which moves a van's sliding door out from the body when the door is opened. The move is necessary when the van has wider-than-stock tires or fender flares (Fig. 13-1). Wide tires are not a subject of this book, and sliding doors are not recommended, so the odds are that you won't need the information that follows.

But we can't take chances. Professional shops are frequently asked about extenders. Van converters use them and need them. So here they are, minority report or not.

First, the mechanism involved. The sliding door rides in a track, just below the drip rail that separates side from roof. There's a "trolley" that rides in the track, and the trolley and door are joined by a link with a complicated hinge at the outboard end of the link (Fig. 13-2). The hinge contains springs, cams, locks, and so forth.

When the door is unlatched and pushed back, the trolley is locked in place and the link swivels, taking the door away from the side of the van. When it's all the way out, nearly at right angles to the track, the hinge locks and the trolley loosens in the track. The door slides back and away from the opening. When the door is pushed forward, the trolley slides forward until it hits a catch, which stops the trolley and releases the hinge, so the rear of the door swings toward and into the opening, until the door latch itself takes over and snugs the door shut.

All we need to do is lengthen the link so the door is farther

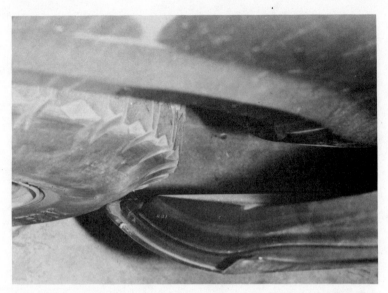

Fig. 13-1. Fat, off-road tires jut past the fender edges. The lower leading edge of a sliding door contacts the tire.

from the body side and thus won't foul the tire or fender. For this, there's a kit that comes from *Taylor Enterprises,* the upholstery and retail shop mentioned in Chapter 2. They developed the kit because they kept getting questions from people whose doors and tires came together.

Fig. 13-2. The link between wall and door is a short, U-shaped piece. The inner end fastens to a sliding car.

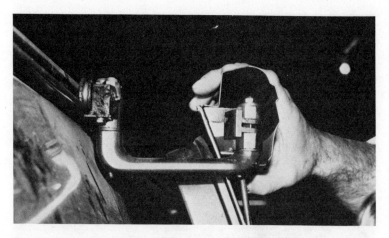

Fig. 13-3. With door edge propped up, remove the link cover and unbolt the outer end. The door and link can be pulled apart. Be careful not to disturb the cams and locks in the sliding and pivoting mechanisms.

The kit has two pieces, a longer-than-stock link and a new stop. The latter is needed because the longer link requires that the trolley stop farther from the door opening than before.

The actual work is a breeze. Caution is the only skill, and hand tools, a hammer, and a jack stand are the only equipment.

Careful now—the locking, latching, cam-and-spring business is devilishly tricky *and must not be disturbed.*

Open the door and slide it out and about halfway back. You want the trolley rolling free and the link locked in the outer position. Remove the covers from the slide and the hinge (Fig. 13-3). Look carefully at the positions of all the pieces, just in case. Place

Fig. 13-4. The door extender kit is simple. A new link, several inches longer than the original, and a new striker plate are all you need.

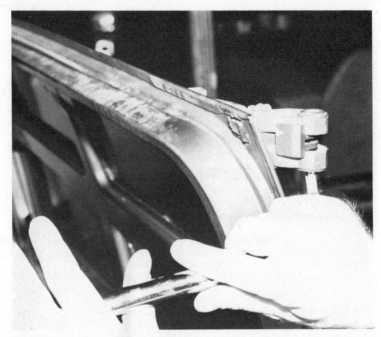

Fig. 13-5. The new link pops right into the old mounting holes and bolts firmly.

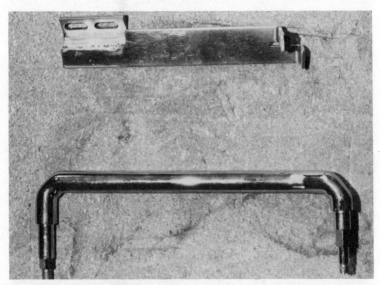

Fig. 13-6. The new striker plate stops the car farther from the door edge and pivots the link and door into closed position. the two bolts at right cover slotted holes that allow adjustments.

the jack stand under the edge of the door, at exactly the height of the door; that is, don't raise it or let it sag.

Undo the nut that holds the outside end of the link (Fig. 13-4) in the hinge. Tap the end of the link out of hinge—nice and easy.

Put the new link into the hinge, again carefully, in order not to disturb the parts (Fig. 13-5). Fit the nut and run it up finger tight.

Undo the old slide where it runs in the track. Remove it and the old link, which is still attached. Push the inboard end of the new link into the new slide—don't worry about telling one end from the other; they are quite different and there's no way this can be down wrong—and put the slide back into the track (Fig. 13-6). Tighten the nut at the inboard end, tighten the nut at the outboard

Fig. 13-7. The door moves farther away from body and tire, and you no longer bang the door into the tire.

end, and screw down the slide in the track. Don't overtighten the screw.

For an eyeball sort of start, you can set the stop far behind the old stop as the new link is longer than the old link. Remove the jack stand. Close the door and see how everything lines up. The stop's mounting holes are slotted, so it can be adjusted back and forth. If the door doesn't close all the way, tap the slide forward a tad. If the front of the door hits the latch, but the rear of the door hasn't swung flush with the body, tap it back. Continue until the door closes perfectly. Replace the hinge and slide covers, and it's all done (Fig. 13-7).

Chapter 14

Music Systems

Few vans today do not have a music or sound-producing component, whether provided with the vehicle or added later. The general driving public craves music or broadcasts to wile away the monotony of driving. Today van and auto stereo is enjoying a popularity boom typical of that experienced about a decade ago in the home audio industry. Auto stereo today can be as sophisticated as home stereo, featuring power boost amps, high output receivers and tape components, audio equalizers, and super speakers producing sound and clarity never before realized or imagined.

A majority of the small autosound components were designed basically with cars in mind, and their inherent sound-producing qualities are quite good. The identical equipment installed in a van boasts even better sound because a van has four to five times the space as a car to provide better acoustic capability and stereophonic presence. This is provided that the van is properly insulated to minimize outside noise caused by wind, engine noise, suspension, and street noise.

Differing from the lower-powered system found in the typical car, a van stereo system must overcome noise and space problems to deliver music of maximum clarity. This can be adequately achieved by using high amplified components and additive power boosters coupled with superior speaker output capabilities. What is considered good amplifier output for a sound-producing component? Up to now, 8 to 12 watts per channel was considered optimum or good, especially for cars. With the newer, larger, power-hungry speakers necessary to provide ultimate sound quality with minimal distortion for a van, 8 to 12 watts is considered poor. For good, distortion-free sounds in vans, a minimum output of 20 watts per channel is necessary. If the existing system does not meet proper requirements, or if a desired receiver or component does not feature high-wattage output, you can add an auxiliary power boost amplifier.

AMPLIFIERS

Most of the contemporary autosound component manufacturers feature auxiliary power boost amps in their catalogs and brochures. Because the larger speakers with their larger magnets require more power than their small 5-inch counterparts, an auxiliary power amp is virtually a necessity unless high wattage is already common to a selected component. Many of today's power-hungry speakers require 10 to 20 watts apiece to produce the lush, full sounds of which they are ultimately capable. If more than two speakers are used within the system, even more power may be required for all-around efficiency (Fig. 14-1).

In the booster amp department, Mitsubishi offers two excellent booster amp modules, the CV-22 and CV-25. The CV-22 provides 25 watts per channel while the CV-25 puts out 25 watts per channel distributed through *four* channel outputs, ideal when four speakers are used within the system. Another Mitsubishi booster component, the CV-23, includes in addition to 30 watts per channel amplification, a graphic equalizer integrated into the unit. These units provide substantial power to feed the newer, more sophisticated speakers.

Sanyo Electric, a leading company offering some of the finest quality both in low budget and top budget lines, markets an excellent minipowerhouse, the PA6030. The miniamp features 15 watts per channel boost and is excellent for upgrading an existing low-watt system. Output jacks that can be used with any component system are included. The PA6030 accepts line level inputs from all Sanyo decks (or other systems) featuring line outputs with a 500 to 1000 MW signal level and speaker level inputs from conventional car decks.

If you want the ultimate power amp, you can't beat the Sanyo PA6110. The amp provides super power with low distortion (0.05 percent harmonic distortion), offering the finest, cleanest sound possible today. Sanyo offers a huge, extensive catalog illustrating

Mitsubishi Model CV-21 (courtesy Mitsubishi)

Sanyo Model PA6030 (courtesy Sanyo)

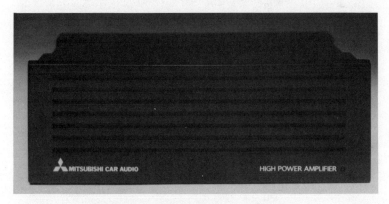

Mitsubishi Model CV-22 (courtesy Mitsubishi)

Fig. 14-1. Power boost amplifiers are almost a requirement for state-of-the-art, optimum sound. Here are some of the better ones.

their complete line that is so impressive and all encompassing it should be perused by every prospective sound component buyer.

Admirable power boost amps are also available from Pioneer (the BP 320 with 12 watts per channel), the Spectron 600 (50 watts per channel), and the Alpine 3008 (30 watts per channel).

The most modern powerhouse amps on the market come from Sansui and Sony. These are optimum car stereo components (see Fig. 14-2).

The Sansui Model SM-100 is priced at $229. It has 32 watts per channel continuous power output into 4 ohms, both channels driven, and from 20 Hz to 20 kHz, with no more than 1.0 percent total harmonic distortion (THD). Its signal-to-noise ratio, per IHF A-200 reference, is 90dB. Frequency response is 20 Hz to 50 kHz, +0dB, −3dB, reference to IHF A-202.

In addition to selectable input levels, the unit features a booster input (for 8 ohms). It also has high/low inputs (RCA jacks) and DIN input for exceptional operational and installation versatility and flexibility. It measures 8 1/4 by 2 1/4 by 8 1/2 inches (w, h, d). It comes in a black finish.

The Sansui SM-50 retails for $99. It has 12 watts per channel power output into 4 ohms, both channels driven, and from 20 Hz to 20 kHz, with no more than 1.0 percent THD. Its signal-to-noise ratio is also 90dB, and its frequency response is also 20 Hz to 50 kHz, per the same IHF reference as the SM-100. Featuring selectable input levels, it measures 3 1/2 by 1 5/8 by 6 1/2 inches (w, h, d). It also comes in a black finish.

A super-powerhouse is the Sansui SM-150 (Fig. 14-3). The SM-150 is four amplifiers in one. Rated output (AD HOC spec) for the unit is 2-×-40 watts rear, 2-×-16 watts front at 1 kHz into 4 ohms, less than 1 percent THD. Frequency response is 20-50,000 Hz, ±3dB with a signal-to-noise ratio of 90dB.

Three types of input connectors are available—Sansui's special DIN connector booster type (special loop) and RCA pin jacks (preamp)—so that the SM-150 connects with any preamp or receiver with provisions for an external power amp. For wide versatility, a Sansui exclusive BDBC (Balanced Differential Booster Circuit) is added to the booster input, which permits any cassette receiver with built-in fader to balance front and rear sounds; no adaptor is required.

The new slim-line XM-E70 equalizer/amplifier from Sony Consumer Products Company combines a high-power amplifier and a seven-band graphic equalizer permitting the listener to fine tune

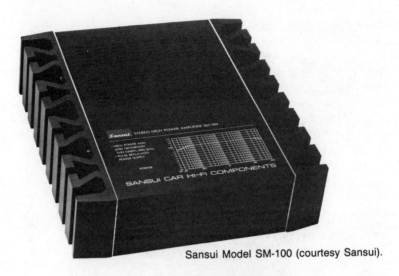

Sansui Model SM-100 (courtesy Sansui).

Sansui Model SM-50 (courtesy Sansui).

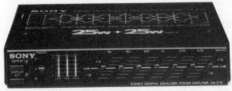

Sony Model XM-E70 (courtesy Sony).

Fig. 14-2. Separate components are the ideal way to go.

Fig. 14-3. The Sansui SM-150 is a super-powerhouse, 4-channel amplifier (courtesy Sansui).

the sound to any car's acoustics and any personal taste.

Engineered with high-tech styling, the XM-E70 has been designed with a three-band power indicator that features pulsating, illuminated graphics for instant visual comparison between low, middle, and high frequencies. Each frequency is represented by a different color LED on the EQ knobs, and each color corresponds to the same color on the power level indicator.

An input level control matches the output of the XM-E70 to the receiver being used. A fader control allows control over the volume of front and rear pairs of speakers.

The XM-E70 also features a defeat switch that bypasses the equalizer to allow an instant comparison between corrected and uncorrected sound without altering the equalizer control setting. The unit measures 7 1/8 inches wide by 1 3/16 inches high by 6 inches deep.

SOUND SOURCE COMPONENTS

Sound source components (AM-FM; cassette) are too numerous to mention, with varied integrated and coordinated items in all possible combinations. One can purchase single tuner, cassette, or equalizer components, or integrated all-in-one units. Combined units are compact, space saving, and economical because they share the same chassis.

For state-of-the-art quality, separate components are the best way to go. Remember that separates involve more discreet and careful installation plus added room. If the van contains an overhead console, this problem is minimized because all the single components can be integrated into an out-of-the-way, attractive, functional housing. In a majority of the vans today, overhead console mounting is rapidly replacing in or under-dash mounting for looks, functionality, and ease of maintenance.

An outstanding and highly recommended all-in-one receiver deck is the TD-700. It is a less expensive, compact counterpart of its predecessor, model TD-1200.

The TD-1200 features a remarkable but expensive auto servo system to accommodate head azimuth alignment. On the other hand, the TD-700 has a knob-operated head azimuth alignment system for best high-frequency response adjustment.

The TD-700 is one of the few receivers to meet or exceed its designated specifications. Its frequency response encompasses a few 31.5 to 18,000 Hz range in both 120 and 70 microsecond standard tapes. Due to its dual capstan drive system, flutter readings are at minimal levels. Its sound and reproduction facilities approach home video quality.

Sansui is again in the big leagues with its magnificent, hard-to-parallel receiver offerings. Its receiver line (Fig. 14-4) encompasses the CX-990, CX-900, RX-710, and RX-510.

The Sansui Model CX-990 is the world's first car stereo "head" unit featuring universal AM stereo broadcasting system selection. The set is a tuner/preamp/cassette player designed for use with an auxiliary power amplifier.

The tuner section of the new CX-990 features quartz synthesizer PLL tuning with 24 presets (18 for FM and 6 for mono or stereo AM). It offers automatic scanning of the 24 preset stations in 5-second intervals for convenient program selection. The station frequencies appear in bright-colored digital form.

Tuner monitoring is another feature of the CS-990. This provides radio music during the interval when the tape transport is rewinding or fast-forwarding a tape. The automatic-reversing transport is IC-logic-controlled for feather-touch operation. Its AMPS (Automatic Music Program Search) allows automatic skip-

Sansui Model CX-990

Sansui Model CX-900

Sansui Model RX-700

Sansui Model RX-500

Fig. 14-4. Sansui offers a fine selection of receivers (courtesy Sansui).

ping to the next selection on a tape to facilitate program selection.

Other features and selling points of the CX-990 are Dolby B and Dolby C noise reduction, dual amp balance, bass and treble controls, and provisions for insertion of an equalizer via the preamp circuitry. Key specifications include FM sensitivity of 14.8dBf for 30dB quieting and 65dB selectivity.

An in-dash head unit is available as a standard sized model (the CX-900) or the larger DIN size model (the CX-910). It features quartz synthesizer PLL tuning, station presets for automatic scanning, AMPS, and an automatic-reversing transport that is IC-logic-controlled. Tape and system noise are kept to a minimum by Dolby B and Dolby C noise-reduction circuits.

The CX-900/910 requires a separate power amplifier for operation. An equalizer can be inserted via the preamp circuitry, bass and treble controls, and four-way dual amp balance controls. Key specifications are FM sensitivity of 14.8dBf for 30dB quieting, selectivity of 50dB, and signal-to-noise ratio of 70dB (mono), 65dB (stereo). The CX-900 measures 7 3/32 × 2 × 4 23/32 inches (w, h, d). The CX-910 measures 7 3/32 × 2 × 5 29/32 inches (w, h, d).

The Sansui models, RX-700 and RX-500, feature quartz synthesizer PLL tuning with presets for 18 FM and 6 AM stations. Each features automatic preset scanning in 5-second intervals until the desired station is found. Both are automatic-reversing units and feature AMPS and soft-touch transport controls. An equalizer can also be inserted via the preamp circuitry bass and treble controls, and four-way fader controls. Each of the models are available in two versions—standard size and in slightly larger DIN size.

Sony engineering has finally developed the technology to eliminate, not mask, the irritating noise of multipath distortion. *Multipath distortion* occurs when direct and reflected PM signals are picked up at a single antenna. To solve this problem, Sony's car stereo XR-100 model uses the Diversity Reception System, two antennas in separate reception locations. The XR-100's microprocessor (Fig. 14-5) constantly monitors the signals coming in from both antennas and selects from the best signal. The switch occurs so fast, it's inaudible. The listener is assured of great sound because he will always receive the best possible signal.

Other key features of the XR-100 include a dual-adjust head, auto-reverse cassette deck with maximum optimum head-to-tape alignment in both directions of tape travel. It also boasts an amorphous tape head found in many top-of-the-line home cassette decks

Fig. 14-5. Sony's Model XR-100 (courtesy Sony).

manufactured by Sony. The hard and resilient head eliminates the noise associated with conventional heads.

Dolby B and C

The XR-100, included in the new high-tech Sony line, also features Dolby B and C. The combination of Dolby B and C reduces tape hiss to dramatically lower levels for accurate sonic reproduction during playback of prerecorded tapes.

The XR-900 and the XR-80 also incorporate a cassette deck that features a narrow gap, hard permalloy head and FG servo motor. The result is an exceptionally low wow and flutter levels—0.07 percent for the XR-900, and 0.09 percent for the XR-80. Like the XR-100, these high-powered units are preamp only.

DIN "E" Sized Receivers

With the growing popularity of new DIN "E" sized receivers, Sony's new receiver line includes three units that fall into this emerging product category. The new DIN "E" sized units are standard size and can be installed in existing in-dash space in almost every American or foreign car. All the new units also feature a built-in quartz clock.

Sony's DIN "E" sized units are the XR-900 (previously described), the XR-780, and the XR-740. The XR-780 has a power output of 20 watts per channel × four and will be available in

March. The XR-740 has a power output of 20 watts per channel × two.

Other new receivers are the XR-66, XR-44, and the XR-33, which offer a full range of player convenience features at popular prices. The XR-66 and XR-44 both offer Dolby B. All three models feature separate bass and treble controls for finely tuned sound.

The XR-30 and XR-20, introduced previously, are among the most in-demand receivers Sony has ever produced. They are mini-sized AM/FM receivers with auto reverse cassette decks that offer high-demand features at a modest price.

Compact Disc Players

Compact disk players not only revolutionized sound in home audio, but are predestined to be the optimum sound reproduction medium for car stereo. The dynamic range of CDs, which gives them their outstanding advantage, measures *more than 90 dB*. CD sound quality is overwhelming, far surpassing analog recording which has dominated cassette recordings. There is a welcome absence of background noise and tape hiss, and the increased dynamic range enhances every nuance of recorded sound.

Riding the wave of CD popularity, the car audio manufacturers are becoming seriously involved in producing in-dash CD units. Sony (the prime innovator), Pioneer, and Mitsubishi are competing for the car-audio market. In 1984, Sony introduced compact disk players for automobiles and recreational vehicles (vans, trucks, etc.), which were highlights of the year in the autosound industry.

The two models developed by Sony are the CDX-5 Compact Disc Player and the CDX-7 AM/FM Compact Disc Player (Fig. 14-6). The Sony CDX-5 and CDX-R7 features major technological advances that make them small enough for car installation and rugged enough to perform reliably despite the shocks, shakes, and temperature extremes of the car environment. New advanced laser optic and LSI technology developed in Sony's own laboratories made the remarkable performance possible.

For example, dynamic range, the key factor in the CD's lifelike sound, is an impressive 90dB. Total harmonic distortion is a low 0.007 percent. These figures are comparable to today's home CD players, as are the other audio specifications of the CDX-5 and CDX-R7.

The CDX-5 is designed to operate with maximum ease and

Sony Model CDX-R7

Sony Model CDX-5

Fig. 14-6. Sony compact disc players are small enough for car installation, yet rugged enough to perform reliably in a car environment (courtesy Sony).

minimum distraction. As the user inserts a disc, it is automatically drawn into position for play. Most controls are feather-touch, and frequently used buttons are conveniently larger.

The CDX-5 makes it easy to find selections. A large Automatic Music Sensor (AMS) button allows the user to skip directly from song to song in either direction. A Music Scan feature runs the disc in forward or reverse at ten times normal speed. Samples of music are heard at normal pitch, but at reduced volume. There are two separate repeat modes for uninterrupted music: one for any individual track, the other for the entire disc. To give a visual representation of the laser's location on the disc, a fluorescent display shows either track number or elapsed time.

The CDX-5 offers preamplifier outputs for connection to a

power amplifier. Preamplifier volume, bass, and treble controls are logically grouped on the left side of the panel.

The new Sony CDX-R7 incorporates both a Compact Disc player and a quartz frequency synthesis AM/FM tuner. The CDX-R7 has most of the track-access features of the CDX-5, including automatic loading, Automatic Music Sensor, and forward and reverse music scan.

The fluorescent display can be switched to show track number or time of day. (In tuner mode, the same display shows station frequency.) An automatic repeat function replays the entire CD automatically, much like the repeat function of an auto reverse cassette deck. Tuning functions include 18 station presets (12 for FM, 6 for AM), automatic scan tuning, manual tuning, FM stereo/mono switching, and FM local/distant switching.

Both new Sony models conform to the new DIN standard for in-dash car stereo units. The chassis mounts easily into most foreign and domestic cars.

Pioneer has handled the mounting feasibility of a CD auto player with a different approach. The Pioneer CDX-1 was introduced in 1985, a year after Sony's introduction. It consists of two separate, coordinating components.

The dual component unit consists of an operating module and a hideaway processing module. The processing module which can be installed in a remote location (there are a multitude in the van), contains the power source and the electronics for converting digital disc information into music. The disc player itself will install easily in virtually all car dashboards and in all vans and trucks.

The Pioneer CDX-1's many convenience features include: music search (2-second access) music scanning, skip searching, and total disc repeat. A specially designed temperature sensing device in the CDX-1 detects changes in temperature and automatically disengages the playback system to prevent possible damage to the laser tracking system.

In the future it is possible that CD in-car players will be the mainstay in autosound, even as factory installed options. Compact discs have been widely and favorably accepted. Their own prohibitive feature is high cost, and this factor too will change in time.

SPEAKERS

Speaker selection and speaker layout should be carefully

thought out and planned. Power capabilities and outputs of speakers and receiver/tape/amp units should be matched to obtain optimum sound from the integrated system. Feeding low-power amp wattage into high-power speakers will result in distortion or "garbled" sound. Better results are sometimes realized by feeding an incoming signal from a powerful amp to a smaller or marginal quality speaker as opposed to pushing a large 6 × 9 or 8-inch speaker with a low 4-watt to 8-watt amp. The basic prerequisite for the best quality is high wattage emanating from the amp to make large, more sophisticated speakers give deep bass response in low frequency areas and distortionless tones on the high end. The more powerful speakers will emit better harmonics throughout their entire range if high-power booster amps are chosen and coordinated according to the efficiency of the speaker.

Ideally, a speaker should reproduce similarly all the varied frequencies transmitted from the amplifier, but this does not always happen. The human ear can span frequencies between 20 cycles and 20,000 cycles. It is impossible for a single speaker with one cone to cover that range. Manufacturers produce speakers with different size cones within one enclosure and coaxials that contain two cones. The woofer cones produce better low tones, the smaller tweeter cones produce better high tones. The better systems are composed of two or three speakers of various sizes in a common enclosure electronically linked together with a crossover network. The crossover network (usually a small box) wired into the speaker system separates the incoming music into the proper frequencies relevant to the proper speakers. Sometimes a third speaker may be included that will span the frequencies between the woofer and tweeter. This is called a *midrange*.

From Spectron comes the 700, featuring a 5-inch woofer and 1-inch dome tweeter. Mitsubishi presents the SX40 SA, a two-way acoustic air suspension system with various tweeter attenuator for precise high frequency adjustment.

An alternative solution to the integrated speaker system is the coaxial speaker. Many are available from Sanyo, Jensen, Mitsubishi, Panasonic, and Pioneer. If you're going the coaxial route, pick a 6 × 9, 8- or 6 1/2-inch that has the tweeter cone mounted directly to the center pole piece (example: Sanyo SP14, Sanyo SP9046H). Coaxials that mount the tweeter by a cross plate over the woofer will not sound as good.

When the tweeter is mounted inside the pole piece of the woofer, no adverse sound reflections can occur, a side effect that exists with a plate mounted across the woofer. The reflections or "bounce-back" waves produce unclean and "garbled" sound called *intermodulation distortion*.

Triaxials are the worst way to go and should not be considered if optimum sound is desired. Triaxials promote more intermodulation distortion that their coaxial equivalents because they block even more of the woofer. Remember that the bounce back waves created by dual tweeters mounted across the woofer will inhibit and subdue bass response.

A question frequently posed pertains to speaker magnet weight. Do bigger magnets provide better sound? Not always, even though magnet size does determine speaker efficiency. Considering two identical speakers with two identical voice coils: if one contains a 5-ounce magnet and the other a 10-ounce magnet, the one with the heavier magnet will take less power from the amplifier, thus making it more efficient. On the other hand, if the 10-ounce magnet must drive a voice coil heavier than the one that the 5-ounce magnet must drive, sound output versus power output may be identical, but with sound and power characteristics differing. A speaker that sounds louder may not sound as clean or as clear as one sounding softer. Your autosound dealer is the one who can best demonstrate this and clue you in on all the existing variances. He can advise you about which speakers can be best applied to an existing sound source component system and can guide you toward putting a well-balanced system together.

Speaker placement should be considered. If possible, mount them so that there are no existing obstructions (seats, cabinets, etc.) between speaker and listener that may disturb sound waves. Popular placement is on front doors, in overhead consoles facing downward, and ideally, high in the rear corners of the van.

Following are examples of the "hot" speaker units and setups that have gained a most favorable following.

The Sony SX-HF2 is a luxury component speaker system featuring high-performance titanium and polypropylene components (Fig. 14-7). Comprised of an SX-H2 titanium dome tweeter and XS-F2 polypropylene full-range speaker, the compact system has multiple mounting flexibility and can be installed virtually anywhere in the car.

The XS-H2 tweeter features a lightweight, 1-inch titanium diaphragm dome that provides the required stiffness for clean, clear highs from 5,000 to 40,000 Hz. A distortion reduction sheet surrounding the diaphragm protects against reflection and reduces

Sony Model XS-HF2 (courtesy Sony).

Sansui Models SB-X903 (left) and SB-X907 (right) (courtesy Sansui).

Sansui Models SB-F703 (left) and SB-F707 (right) (courtesy Sansui).

Fig. 14-7. Speakers come in all sizes and configurations. They should be chosen with the ears, not the eyes.

distortion. A high-energy magnet results in full-spectrum frequency with strength and ultra-low distortion.

The XS-F2 full-range speaker uses a 5 1/4-inch polypropylene cone for full-spectrum, high-fidelity sound and excellent resonance. Polypropylene's consistency also makes it impervious to moisture, which can cause damage to cones made of paper. In addition, a copper short-ring surrounds the ferrite magnet to reduce distortion. Frequency response ranges from 75 to 12,000 Hz. An attractive, acoustically transparent metal grille protects speakers, and Sony supplies a mounting adaptor for easy installation in areas only 1 3/8 inches deep.

Optimum sound procedures on the Sansui roster are the SB-X907, SB-X903, SB-F-707, and SB-F-703. All are three-way systems of the highest calibre (see Fig. 14-7).

At the top of the line is the three-way Model SB-X907. It utilizes a 5 1/8-inch woofer, dual-passive radiator, a 2 1/2-inch midrange, and 1-inch tweeter. Its cabinet is of die-cast aluminum. It can handle up to 100 watts of power. Frequency response is 43 Hz to 22 kHz, plus/minus 2dB.

Model SB-X903, utilizes a 4 3/4-inch woofer and dual-passive radiator, a 2-inch midrange plus a 1-inch tweeter, all mounted in an ABS high-impact plastic cabinet. It can handle up to 80 watts of power. Its frequency response is 55 Hz to 21 kHz, plus/minus 2dB.

Two three-way models meant for flush-mount rear deck installation feature Sansui's "FlexAxis" tweeter. This 1-inch tweeter, mounted above the frame, permits the user to "aim" the high-frequency response for the most pleasing and accurate sound. Model SB-F707, priced at $269 per pair, features an 8-inch round woofer, 2 1/2-inch midrange, and 1-inch tweeter. It can handle up to 70 watts of power. Frequency response is 28 Hz to 22 kHz, plus/minus 2dB. It requires 3 inches of mounting depth. Model SB-F703, priced at $199 per pair, features a 6 1/2-inch round woofer, 2-inch midrange, and 1-inch tweeter. Its power handling capacity is 60 watts. Its frequency response is 38 Hz to 22 kHz, plus/minus 2dB. Minimum required mounting depth is 2 1/2 inches.

Three other commendable models from Sansui are the SB-135, SB-690, and SB-1100 (Fig. 14-8). The SB-135, a 5 1/4-inch speaker, features a very narrow mounting depth (only 1 25/32 inch) and can handle 40 watts of power with frequency response of 40 to 21,000 Hz.

Sansui Model SB-690 is a two-way 6- x -9-inch rear speaker with

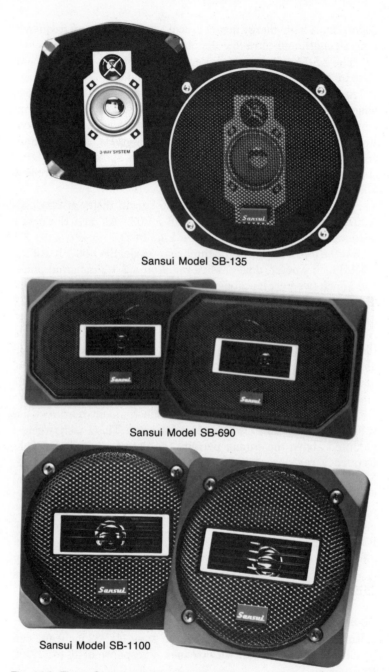

Sansui Model SB-135

Sansui Model SB-690

Sansui Model SB-1100

Fig. 14-8. These Sansui speaker systems take up a minimum of space and still provide superb performance (courtesy Sansui).

146

10-ounce magnet, 60 watts power handling capability, 92 dB/m/w sensitivity, and frequency response of 35 to 20,000 Hz. Its mounting depth is 3/4 inch and its oval grille measures approximately 10 × 6 1/2 inches.

Model SB-1100 is a 4-inch, dual-cone door speaker with a maximum input capacity of 25 watts, sensitivity of 89 dB/m/w, and frequency response of 50 to 19,000 Hz. Its magnet weighs 5.3 ounces and its mounting depth is 1 1/4 inches. It comes with a 4 3/4-inch round grille.

For the custom audiophile and sound connoisseur, a simple but effective speaker installation is illustrated in Figs. 14-9 to 14-15. This is highly effective and is utilized in the Badger Star Bus featured in Chapter 22. The installation is very favorable because the necessary components are not too costly. Speaker components of the type shown may be obtained at a local Radio Shack dealer. Total expenditure should not exceed $80 (Fig. 14-9).

All that is necessary to undertake this project is a piece of 3/4-inch plywood to serve as the baffle board and a good jigsaw (Fig. 14-10). Cutting and fitting the baffle board (rear quarters of vans vary in size) is the initial step. Prior to mounting the baffle, the speakers and crossover network are installed (Figs. 14-11 and 14-12). This piece should be mounted diagonally across the rear ceiling to the door frame corner. The procedure is simple. The results are very effective with excellent tonal quality and magnifi-

Fig. 14-9. To build a ceiling baffle system, purchase the following components: one 8-inch woofer, one 3-inch tweeter, and appropriate crossover network.

Fig. 14-10. After measurements inside the van are taken, a baffle board is cut to size and fit in as shown.

cent response throughout the entire harmonic range. To guard against sound wave bounce-back from the van's metal skin, an overall 1/2-inch thick piece of foam rubber was contact cemented

Fig. 14-11. Place the speakers in their respective positions, calculate and draw the opening sizes, and cut out the openings with a jigsaw.

Fig. 14-12. Secure the speakers with wood screws and wire according to instruction sheet provided with speakers and crossover network.

Fig. 14-13. The final assembly is secured into the ceiling. A 3-inch spacer block is mounted across the ceiling toward the front of the baffle board to allow some acoustic space behind the baffle. The finished piece may be covered with grille cloth or other decorative material.

149

Fig. 14-14. When components are all contained in an overhead console, most of the wiring can be localized for easy, trouble-free maintenance.

to the van metal behind the baffle (Figs. 14-14 and 14-15).

When choosing or considering your ideal sound system, we advise that your ears, and not your eyes, be the final judge (Fig. 14-16). You should consult your autosound dealer. He can best advise you and in most instances will be most eager to demonstrate the components in which you are interested.

Fig. 14-15. Typical overhead console component installation.

Fig. 14-16. Let your ears be the judge when choosing sound components. Your dealer is equipped to provide demonstrations.

Chapter 15

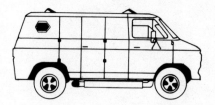

Tables

Van converters who like to eat inside their mobile quarters won't need much convincing when it comes to removable tables. If you eat inside and don't have a table, you eat on your lap—awkwardly. Tables are nice to have (Fig. 15-1). They are also easy to make and install. The basic parts are a mounting plate with socket for the floor, a steel tube to slip into the socket and into the bottom of the table, another mounting plate and socket for the table underside, and the table itself, which can be any size and shape you like.

The metal parts are available from RV equipment stores, van-conversion shops, and the better mail-order camping equipment places. All brands seem to come in pretty much the same size, and any size or shape you choose is string enough to bear the weight. There can be a problem with height, as the comfortable height of table from floor will depend on the height of the seats, and that varies with the builder of the van. When you buy a complete set, i.e., sockets and post, you'll get a post of average length. Usually the ends are tapered to fit into the socket without hassle. Plan ahead. The catalog lists the post's length. If you know the height of the seats, you'll know if the set will work, or whether you'll have to buy the sockets separately and get the post from a plumber or sheet metal shop. Nothing to it, either way.

Equal care is needed to properly place the floor socket. If the table will go between two seats or the two halves of a UniLounge, the socket should go exactly between them. You have a choice of

Fig. 15-1. Removable tables are neat and easy to install.

Fig. 15-2. The table base can be installed on the floor, atop the rug, as shown, or beneath it. Legs come in standard sizes and can be trimmed if the table is too high.

sequence here. If the van has a wood panel on the floor, mount the socket after the wood and before the rug. Use heavy sheet metal screws, and if they go through the wood into the metal, so much the better. If the floor gets foam padding, locate and mount the socket on the bare metal, then install padding and rug around the base. If the table is chosen after the rug is down, pick the best place and mark the spot with an "X" slashed in the rug. Peel the four triangles back, remove the padding, install the base, and glue the

Fig. 15-3. Assembly is as logical as it looks.

Fig. 15-4. The socket for the bottom of the table attaches with wood screws, via guide holes drilled with the socket as a pattern. Put the socket in the center of the table.

rug edges back over. You can put the base on top of the carpet (Fig. 15-2). It will work fairly well with the indoor/outdoor variety, but shag is sure to compress unevenly and leave the table at a tilt. Plan ahead, as always.

The post just slips into the sockets. The table-side socket mounts on the table underside with wood screws (Fig. 15-3). For pride in workmanship, align the socket with the table's edges, even though nobody will ever notice, and the table will square up with the seats because it will swivel in its sockets (Fig. 15-4).

The tabletop itself requires woodworking. The actual choices are legion, but they all must be made by the builder himself. There doesn't seem to be any tabletops sold retail—presumably because the table size depends on the van and the floor plan—and no two are alike.

A nice piece of hardwood, 1 inch thick and carefully oiled, var-

155

Fig. 15-5. The tabletop can be shaped for fashion or to fit whatever floor plan you wish. This passenger seat has been mounted aft of normal position and swivels to match the table.

nished, polished, rubbed, and whatever, is the usual choice. But you can use softwood and cover the top with tile, vinyl, Formica—just about any material. The edges can be finished like any other piece of furniture, or you can trim them with plastic and metal strips from the do-it-yourself store. There are more options here than can be listed.

Dimensions are also up to the builder. Generally, the table will be a rectangle, almost as long as the seats it serves and wide enough to slightly overlap the seat front; that is, close enough to be reached without stretching. But home builders have made round, square, triangular, and octagonal tables, depending on floor plan and personal taste (Fig. 15-5).

Chapter 16

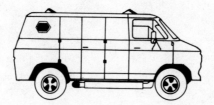

Seats

Custom seats are probably the most natural improvement made to vans, whether the vehicle is to be used for camping, hauling, or cruising. There are two reasons for this.

The first is that vans were supposed to be commercial vehicles, bought for business by men who'd never drive the things. Price and cost are far more important than comfort to that type of buyer. So, van seats are spartan. They are designed to stand up under hard use and not to be used in comfort. Window vans have the same basic seats, but they are covered with better fabric and are less drab. Even so, stock seats can use improvement.

Second, the sets are easily replaced. The factories use a tubing framework below the seat proper. Captive nuts are set in the floor, and bolts attach the framework. The bolts are easy to reach, so the seats can be removed quickly. The makers of custom seats always design their van models to mount with original nuts. Removal and replacement can be done in half an hour.

TYPES

Choosing the seats will take more time than that. The types available are many—indeed, there seems to be a new idea made public every day. A complete catalog isn't possible here, but we can look at and discuss some general types.

Most popular is the *highback seat*. As the name implies, it has a high back with a headrest incorporated. Highbacks are usually

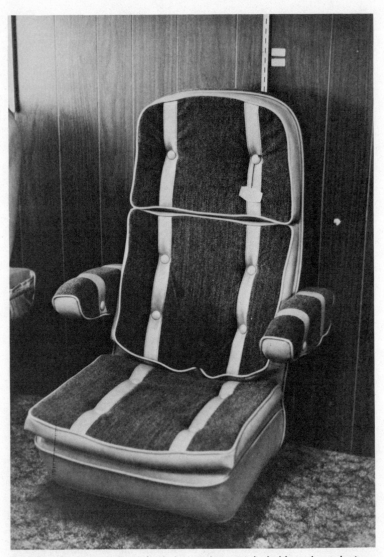

Fig. 16-1. Cushioned captain's chairs are the most desirable and popular type of seating today. These are covered in fabric and Naugahyde (courtesy Florida Van Seats).

made with the stock seat as the starting point. The conversion shop strips off the fabric and padding and welds a headrest frame onto the top of the original frame. Then the padding is replaced and added to, and the seat is covered with vinyl, fabric, or a combination of the two. There's no limit to color. It you don't see what you want, ask. Most shops will happily redo a pair of sets in any color you want.

A *captain's chair* carries the conversion one step further (Fig. 16-1). The name used here comes from dining room furniture, sets of which are designed with plain chairs for the family and chairs with armrest for the heads for the table. A captain's chair, then, is a highback with armrests. The frame is modified to take these armrests, which can be either lowered to horizontal or raised to fit into recesses in the seat back.

From there the choice advanced to the *reclining seat.* Still the general size and shape of the highback, the recliner has had the back and cushion frames reworked into sort of a giant hinge, and the back is adjustable from bolt upright to full recline. It is a nice feature, because minute variations in backrest angle can do wonders for the spine on a long drive.

The *custom highback seat* can also be bought with a new lower frame that allows the seat to swivel. In passenger cars swiveling seats were once used to make entrances and exits easier. In vans there's more to be gained because the swiveling seats can be turned halfway around to face a dinette table. (Also, I suspect, it's a feature that the proud owner can show off.)

The *swivel seat* has a large, short tube attached to the bottom of the frame. With the seat comes a new mounting plate consisting

Fig. 16-2. The swiveling seat has two halves in its base. One tube slides over the other, with a clamp to keep the parts stationary. The lever controls the clamp.

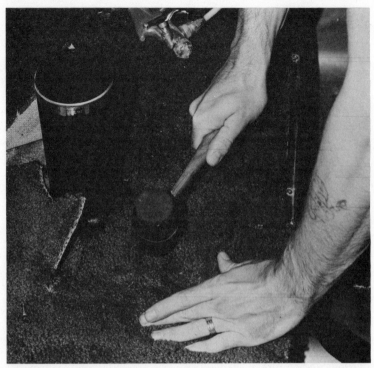

Fig. 16-3. The seat base should be installed before the carpet. When the carpet is trimmed for size, a large "X" marks the seat location. When the carpet is in place, glue down the flaps and trim away the excess.

of a smaller tube, with an outer diameter that matches the seat tube's inner diameter and a flat steel plate to which the tube is welded (Fig. 16-2). The plate is drilled to match the pattern of the captive bolts on the floor.

Swivel seats swivel by virtue of a clamp arrangement. The upper, outer tube is slotted and can be squeezed by a built-in clamp. The clamp is controlled by a lever below the seat cushion. Reclining seats work in much the same way and is the more expensive of either type. There's provision to move the seat forward and backward, just as in original equipment.

Fancier still is the *barrel seat,* named because of its looks. The barrel seat has a curved back and deep sides, like some living room chairs. The framework is made just for this application rather than being adapted from stock parts. Those made for vans come with mounts to fit the captive nuts on the floor.

Note for those doing interior: plan ahead, as always. If the seat will go on a floor with rug and foam, cut a rectangle out of the foam, slightly larger than the mounting plate, when you install it. Don't put glue on the floor within the square formed by the mounting holes. When the rug is in place, you can locate the seat position by the indentation. Slice a large "X," top-left mounting hole to bottom-right, top-right, to bottom-left. Fold the rug flaps away, slide the plate into place, both it down, spray glue on the underside of the flaps, and press the rug into position (Fig. 16-3). The inner corners will curl up around the tube. Trim them off at floor height. This applies for wood floors, too.

Another note: van manufacturers do not use the same dimensions, so when you order a seat, be sure you specify year and brand. Or, if you get a deal secondhand, be prepared to redrill the plate or have a different plate made.

At the top of the pile, so to speak, are the custom seats designed for long-haul trucks. *Bostrom* is the big name in this field. Bostrom produces seats with their own suspension, plus adjustments for height, rake, swivel, etc. These seats are expensive and overdesigned in the sense that they are built for conditions and uses far more severe than the converted van will put them to.

As a rule the seats today are far superior to the ones produced in the early custom van days. Simple captain's chairs with straight

Fig. 16-4. Finding seats is no more difficult than finding a store dealing in van equipment. Here is a sample of the stock found in a randomly chosen store.

Fig. 16-5. Custom designed seats for this interior were designed and built by Frank of Florida Van Seats, Fort Lauderdale, Florida.

highbacks have given way to cushioned, designer-types that are plusher and far more comfortable. Fine quality swivel and reclining seats are manufactured by Goshen Cushion Inc., Goshen, Indiana, and Florida Van Seats, Fort Lauderdale, Florida. These improved, modern types offer the ultimate in both looks and comfort.

In general, the fancier the seat, the wider. Remember this while shopping. Many an unwary converter has learned too late that he can't swivel the seat because it hits the doorjamb, that the reclining back is blocked by galley cabinet, etc.

SUPPLIERS

When selecting seats remember that seats are bulky and heavy. Many mail-order outfits don't carry them. Most firms specializing in camping gear assume the converter will retain his stock seats, so they don't have custom models.

Cruising-van suppliers have them. Some of the better shops have literally row on row of seats in all styles and colors (Fig. 16-4). Check your neighborhood store and the ads in the van magazines. Converters in rural areas may find this difficult, but after that first long ride in a padded and shaped custom seat, the effort will have paid dividends.

Your local dealer, even if limited in stock, can help you choose and coordinate proper seating for your van. If he does not stock floor samples, he will at least have brochures and pictures of the seats he recommends and sells. He will also have fabric samples on hand so you can choose and properly match seating to your existing or proposed decor. Be sure to obtain the proper pedestals because Ford, Chevy, and Dodge seat mounting differs. If possible, test the seats for comfort and spaciousness to ensure that you have chosen ideal seating (Fig. 16-5).

Chapter 17

Luggage Racks

Big box though it is, your van may not always be big enough to accommodate everything you wish to take. Or there may be things you need to take that get in the way of the people and activities occupying the interior. To solve this problem, we have the luggage rack.

This is an easy project. A luggage rack is simply a set of low railings at the rear and sides of the roof. The three sides form a space on which to rest tents, sleeping bags, boxes, or whatever. You wedge the excess baggage against and between the railings, then you lash all the stuff down with rope or elastic cord. It's convenient once you get used to driving along with your worldly goods subject to the wind; that is, once you have confidence that your straps and ropes will hold, you'll find the rack a handy thing to have.

Luggage racks are popular accessories, so once again the better RV, van, or camping stores stock them. Most of the makers have semiuniversal models, with different sizes for vans and station wagons, but without the need to supply a different model for each make. The only dimension that could matter is the width of the roof, and all three makes of vans are virtually identical in that respect.

First step is to assemble the rack on the ground. The rails are steel or aluminum tubing with slip joints. Most racks have five L-shaped stanchions and two stanchions, which are more like mounting plates with hollow tops into which the tubing will fit. The

Fig. 17-1. The end section of the rail should be positioned at the end of the roof, with center support in exact center, before the holes are drilled.

front tubes are bent to curve down to these mounting plates and the rear tube has two right-angle bends for the corners.

Push the sections of tubing together and slide the L-shaped stanchions onto the tubing with the foot facing in. Position one stanchion at the center rear, two at the joint of rear and side tubes, and the last two at the middle of each side tube. All the pieces should be a light press fit: loose enough to go into place by hand, but firm enough not to fall off as you do the rest of the work.

Put the assembled rack on the roof. The rear stanchion should be 6 inches forward of the rear edge of the roof and in the exact center (Fig. 17-1). Put the tube bases over the ends of the side tubes and position them so each is the same distance from the drip rail at the side of the roof (Fig. 17-2).

If a helper is available, he or she should hold the rack in place. If not, use a couple of long strips of masking tape, one at each side

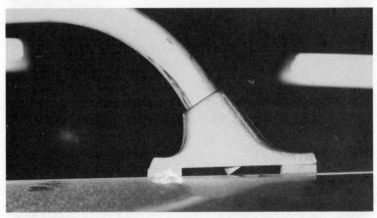

Fig. 17-2. Rail ends into the end stanchions. No clamps or fasteners are needed.

of the center stanchion. This is for security more than anything else, because the rack isn't bearing any weight and shouldn't slip. To be safe, the tape will hold the rack while you drill a 1/8-inch hole, using the rear hole of the center stanchion as a guide. Put a 3/4-inch No. 10 screw in the hole and tighten it.

With the rack now secured by the center stanchion, move on to the next. Drill one hole, insert a screw, etc., checking the alignment each time.

When the rack has been attached at all of its mounting points, go around again and drill the rest of the holes. You might insert the screw each time to be sure the holes are in the right places, but don't bother tightening them.

All holes drilled? Fine. Now remove all the screws and lift the rack off the roof. Any time you drill into the roof, you risk a leak, either from water sitting up there or from water being forced into cracks while you're under way in wet weather. Every hole in the roof should be sealed (Fig. 17-3). You can do this with small pieces of gum tape or with silicon rubber sealant from Dow or GE. Any hardware store has it. Ask for the clear sealer.

Put the gum tape or sealer on the base of each stanchion and tube base. Be generous. Most of the stuff will be squeezed out, but

Fig. 17-3. The stanchion screws, and anyplace where anything goes through the roof metal, should be sealed with gum tape or silicone sealer to keep water out.

Fig. 17-4. The finished rack is barely noticeable and adds enormously to the van's storage capacity.

you want to be sure there's enough to be forced into the holes and to fill any low spots and seams.

When the sealer is in place, put the rack back on the roof. You don't want to spread the sealer around any more than you can help. Insert the screws and tighten them all. No need to use a pattern here, as the fit of stanchion to tube isn't tight and pulling one down firm won't distort or pull the others. When the rack is secure, let the sealer or gum turn tacky, then scrape off the excess with a knife or razor blade.

All you need now (Fig. 17-4) are the luggage and the rope.

Chapter 18

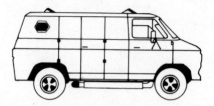

Driving Lights

This is a highly optional sort of project. We are working with van conversions, and vans are more to be lived in than driven. They are not high-speed vehicles, so it follows that the normal lighting system will be adequate for most conditions.

There are vans used for camping in rough country, however. For driving on strange, unpaved roads in the dark, nothing beats a set of extra lights. There are also accessory lights for driving in fog.

Basically there are two types of accessory driving lights. One produces a narrow beam that goes a long way—the *driving light.* The other has a flat, wide beam that spreads across the road and doesn't reach far in front of the vehicle—the *fog lamp.* There are two types of construction for both driving and fog lamps. One uses a sealed unit like the standard headlight in U.S. cars but smaller; the other has a separate bulb and reflector. The bulb element is quartz, treated with iodine, and such lights are known as quartz—iodine, quartz—halogen or Q-I lights. They are new and very powerful. Consequently Q-I lights draw more current than sealed-beam lights, and they are not legal in all states.

Step one should be to check the vehicle code in your state. Some allow anything, some have limits on type and candlepower, and one or two states allow no changes at all.

If it's allowed, pick Q-I lights. They are super. Your van probably has an alternator, so current demand will be no problem. If you're limited to sealed beams, skip the driving lights. They won't give you any more long-distance vision than you get from high-beam and standard lights. Sealed-beam fog lamps, though, can be worthwhile.

White for lamps or yellow? It's been a question for years. It may depend on the user's vision. I prefer (and use) a fog lamp so white it's nearly blue, but if you feel better with yellow, use it.

Finding extra lights is no worry. Sport car, dune buggy, and off road people have been fitting extra lights for years, and almost any parts store dealing with imports has a good selection. As for brand, any name you've heard before will do. Again, personal opinion, but I've been delighted with my Lucas *Square Eights*.

Where to put them? More opinions. Off road lights work best when mounted as high as practical. You're looking for rocks and chuckholes, etc., and they show up better when the light is at an angle to the ground. The roof mount is no showoff stunt. Topless off road racing cars mount their lights on the rollbars, simply to get them as high as they can.

Driving lights seem to be equally effective high or low, and they're usually set above or below the bumper, either mounted on the gravel tray (if there is one) or on the bumper brackets (Fig. 18-1). Accessory lights have a socket affair welded to the lamp body and a bolt through a hole in the hemispherical socket. You slide the

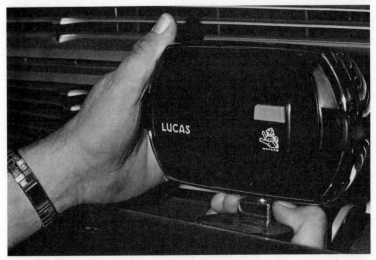

Fig. 18-1. The gravel pan between grille and bumper is the easiest place to put extra lights. This is a Lucas quartz-halogen unit. The light colored panel in the cover glows if the light is left burning or is turned on by accident.

169

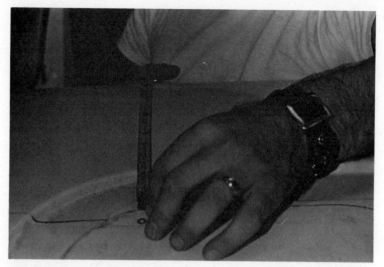

Fig. 18-2. Be careful in locating rooftop light. A line across the roof and two lines back from a point equidistant from each drip rail locates the light.

both through the mounting hole, swivel, or tilt until the light is aimed right, and tighten.

Fog lamps work best when close to the road. Fog hangs above the ground, so the light slips beneath the fog and lights up the ground, while the higher beam would only dazzle itself to death. Under the bumper is the only way.

INSTALLATION

Installation is pretty much universal. We'll proceed on the assumption that lights under the bumper are attached the same way they're attached to the roof.

The precise location isn't critical. Be sure both lights are aligned with each other. Put a tape measure on the drip rail and mark a few inches back from the forward curve on both sides (Fig. 18-2). Run a string across the roof, from one mark to the other. Draw that line with a grease pencil. Measure in from each rail, say 8 inches, so the marks you just made are away from the edge of the roof and almost horizontal. (Too steep an angle and there won't be enough tilt to let the light shine straight ahead.)

Remove the front headliner panel. Drill a hole (3/8 inch or whatever the bolt is) at the marked spot. The mounting bolt is long, for good reason. Put a large metal washer, then a rubber washer, on the bolt. Put the bolt into the hole. Fit another large washer, then the nut. The washers, both metal and rubber, are to prevent squeaks and leaks later on (Fig. 18-3). Leave the nut finger-tight for now and smear some silicone sealer, 3M, Dow, or whatever, around the light base and the outside washers, also to prevent leaks. The light is installed.

That's the easy part. The wires need a hole of their own, as small as is practical. If you can find a rubber grommet that will work, use it. If not, wrap the wires in duct tape where they go through the roof, then cover both sides of the hole with sealer (Fig. 18-4). You don't want any spaces, and you want some protection in case the wire chafes against the metal edge.

Routing the wires from a bumper mount is obviously simple. The roof mount is harder. The lights come with about 1 foot of wire, so you'll need more of whatever gauge the light manufacturer used.

Van makers use the left windshield pillar for the wires to the interior. So can you. Loosen the rubber gasket on the inside of the windshield and on the left side of the instrument panel, then push the new wires down alongside the existing ones.

Tip: You can make four wires into three by joining the two ground wires. Run the right-hand ground wire over to the left light, make a splice, and let one wire ground both lights.

Second Tip: Don't ground the lights to the roof. True, that would

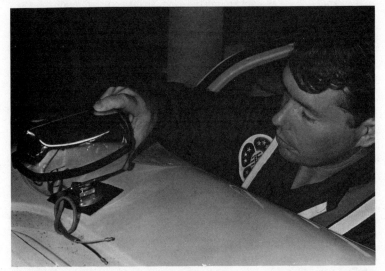

Fig. 18-3. The light base can be insulated from the metal roof with a thin square of rubber. When the light is firmly fastened, trim away the excess rubber.

171

Fig. 18-4. Here's the inside of a rooftop mount. Note the large washer between roof and nut and the sealant around the wires as they come through the roof.

save bother routing wires, but in case of trouble later you couldn't check the circuit without removing the headliner panel.

Solder on the terminal and pick any convenient small screw or bolt on the inside of the dashboard or firewall. It doesn't matter. All you need is a ground that can be reached for troubleshooting.

Switches vary with brand of lamp and with your preference, i.e., toggle, twist, push, or what have you. They can be placed almost anywhere on the instrument panel. The switches shown are the rocker type, set on the panel's upper left. How you install the switches depends on the type. For some, drill a large hole. For switches like the ones shown, you'll have to cut a rectangle out of the panel. Trace the pattern, drill a starter hole, and use a hand-held blade for the rest (Figs. 18-5 and 18-6). (Sorry if that sounds too brisk. I am assuming you're reading this after having installed portholes and vents, and cutting small holes holds no terror for you.)

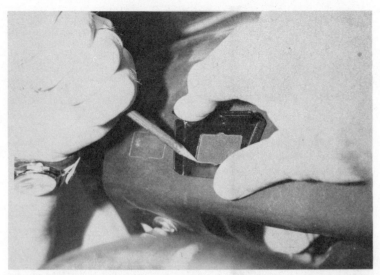

Fig. 18-5. Large switches are a bother. Mark the hole to be cut, using the switch cover plate as a template.

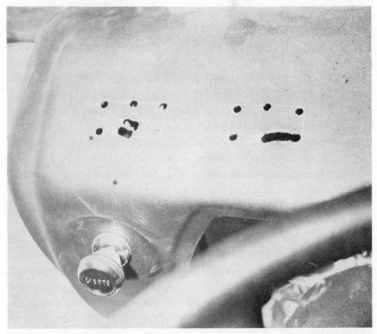

Fig. 18-6. Drill a series of holes along the marked line. The panel is plastic and the holes can be joined with a handsaw or by pushing the drill sideways.

173

Fig. 18-7. Wires are tricky. This shop finds its easiest to remove the instrument panel when reworking wires under the dash.

The switches are ready. All they do is transmit current to the lights from a power source.

This is the hard part (Fig. 18-7). There are several ways to wire accessory lights, and they vary with need and the installer's character. The quickest way is to fit a blade connection to the hot wire from the switch and stuff it into the fuse box, adjacent to the heater motor or some other accessory fuse. This has the virtue of making the extra light independent of the original lighting system.

Independence is also a drawback. You can spend a lot of time throwing switches and dazzling oncoming cars.

The optimum is to tie the new lights into the old wiring network. Your van has a three-position light switch: *off, partial* (with taillights and parking lights only), and *on* (with headlights coming on and parking and taillights staying on).

This can be used to advantage. Run the fog-light hot wire to the switch terminal for the parking lights. Splice it in, or there may be a spare fitting on the switch. Now when you put the light switch to partial, you also activate the fog-light switch. Switch off, same as ever. Fog-light switch on, and you get fog lights with the running lights. And the fog lights stay on when you turn on the headlights.

Driving lights are too powerful to be used in ordinary driving. They are best suited to use with high-beam headlights.

Your van has a dimmer switch. Route the driving light's switch wire to the dimmer switch and splice it into the high-beam terminal. (The markings vary. You'll have to find it by tracing and testing.)

This works like the fog lights. The power comes only when the dimmer switch is in the high position, and it goes to the new switch, which may be on or off. You can run both high beams and driving lights, or just high beams. Best of all, when you see an on-coming car, a jab at the dimmer switch lowers the headlight beams and turns off the driving lights. This is my system, by the way, and I've had great luck with it. I've been using if four years now and never had so much as a warning from the authorities, despite the fact that in my home state, Q-I lights are . . . but perhaps I'd better not tell you about that.

AIMING

Aiming the lights is the last step, and it's best left until nearly all the other projects are completed (Fig. 18-8). Conversions add weight in the rear, and tilting the van naturally causes the lights to aim higher than when everything was stock.

Fog lights have short, flat beams and work best when aimed straight ahead. Driving light beams are long and narrow—*pencil*

Fig. 18-8. This van has a new hood, custom grille, nerf bar instead of bumpers, and a pair of quartz-halogen driving lights on the bar bracket. Effective, but vulnerable.

beams, as they say. Bumper-mounted driving lights should be set straight ahead. For a roof mount, the beams should angle down, meeting the pavement just as the beam loses power. To do this, you need a dead straight, flat road, at night. The adjustment is made by slacking off on the mounting nut and aiming the light, then tightening the nut, making sure the light hasn't moved, doing it again, etc. It can be a one-man job, but like so many others, it's easiest with one man sitting behind the wheel and watching, the other outside doing the work. When they're right, retighten.

Chapter 19

Fender Flares, Running Boards, and Custom Grilles

A van with stock or standard-sized tires and wheels has no need of extended fenders, mud flaps, and the like. But a van with wider wheels, fatter tires, or any suspension modification that puts the tires farther away from the vehicle's centerline, or extends the tread beyond the body sides, may need to cover the exposed treads. There are several reasons. First, it's neater. Uncovered tires throw mud, grit, and such up onto the body and make for a dirty van. Next, politeness. The same spray goes onto other cars. Finally, several states vehicle codes require the treads to be covered, for the reasons mentioned.

This used to be a bothersome and expensive business, requiring metalwork or fiberglass shaping, bonding, blending, and painting. When I began this book, that's the way things stood—and that's why I promised not to get into body modifications. They are too much even for builders who can handle the other projects included.

But at midbook there arrived an easy answer to this. The proper name is *Tire Lips*. They're durable, molded-rubber extensions, adding 2 1/2 inches to the outside edge of each fender. The lips fasten to the inside of the metal opening, so none of the bolts are visible. Further, the work can be done with simple hand tools and an electric drill, which presumably the van converter already owns by now.

FLARES

Flares, whether molded rubber, fiberglass, or ABS, are made for all current vans (Ford, Chevy, Dodge) and may be obtained for model years going back to the early seventies. They are sold in sets of four. When ordering or purchasing from the local dealer, specify van and year. Installation is simple and virtually foolproof.

The first step is to jack up one corner of the van and remove that wheel. Locate the center of the fender edge—you can eyeball this—it isn't critical. Mark the center of one extension and match that center point with the fender edge's center point. When you put the lip in place, there will be gobs of extra material hanging down past the fender at each end. Don't worry about it.

The lip has an edge—that is, there's a right-angle groove running the length of the lip. The narrow side goes inside the fender opening, the wide side extends past the fender, and the groove snugs up against the lip and edge of the metal.

The first screw and washer attach at the center parts (Fig. 19-1). Hold the lip against the fender with one hand and drill the appropriate hole with the other. Then insert screw and washer and fasten firmly.

It would be nice to have a helper handy, so one person can hold the lip in place while the other drills the hole. It would also speed things up to have two drills, one with drill bit and the other with a screwdriving attachment.

You can drill all the holes and then insert all the screws, but

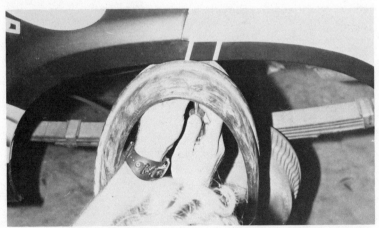

Fig. 19-1. With the van jacked up and the tire removed, begin by placing the middle of the lip in the middle of the wheel opening. Then attach the first screw.

it's risky. The screws go in at 3-inch intervals. This isn't done for strength, but to keep the lip smooth all the way around the fender edge. When you drill and fasten one screw at a time, you can be sure the holes will all be where you want them. A series of empty holes may mean misalignment, and that probably means a wrinkle or a new hole. Take your time.

With the center fastened, work toward both ends, one side at a time (Figs. 19-2 and 19-3). The lips are rubber and excess torque can cause little ripples. If they pop, back off on the screw.

The braces are another option. They come drilled in one end and should be used in place of the washer when you come to a sharp or compound curve. Conforming the groove to an irregular curve in the fender may push the lip into an awkward shape. The brace backs up the screw at the nearest point to this odd shape and can be bent so it pushes the lip into a normal curve. Possibly you won't need to use any braces, as most vans have a fairly regular shaped wheel opening. Just in case, though, the maker gives you plenty.

Ditto the length of each lip. When you finish with the screws, and have gone as far as the metal goes, you'll have excess tire lip. Don't cut it yet. Figure just how far you want the lip to go, usually to the point where the fender edge rolls into the body proper.

The templates are on a sheet. They have one short straight side, one long straight side, and one gradual curve. Peel off the backing and place the template with the short side against the seam of the

Fig. 19-2. Work toward the ends, pressing the lip into place and fastening so the lip conforms to the metal rim.

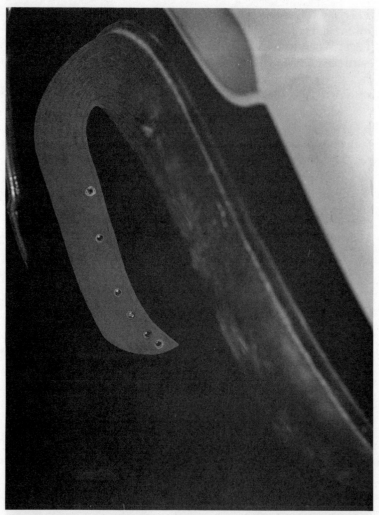

Fig. 19-3. The inside shows a row of screws and washers holding the lip to fender. When the curve gets tricky, place the screws close together.

lip and the long side at the top. The curved edge will be at the lower outside (Fig. 19-4).

Use the razor blade to make a light, smooth cut along the curved line (Fig. 19-5). When you get to the seam, make a cut straight across to the lip's inside.

Peel off the template and finish the cut along the line. When the excess has been removed, use the sandpaper to smooth any jagged edges. For a final touch, spray the screws with black paint.

This makes them nearly impossible to see and prevents corrosion. Now you're clean and legal (Fig. 19-6).

The more discriminating or show van owner may want to mold in his flares so that they do not have that stuck-on look, but appear as an integral part of the van's wheel well (Fig. 19-7). You can do the job yourself with body filler, files, and sandpaper, or you can take it to the local body shop where the job can be done quickly perfectly, and at a not-too-prohibitive cost (Fig. 19-8).

RUNNING BOARDS

Running boards are becoming very popular today, used by themselves or in conjunction with flares. Imaginary Glass, Anaheim, California , a leading manufacturer of quality fiberglass flares, also

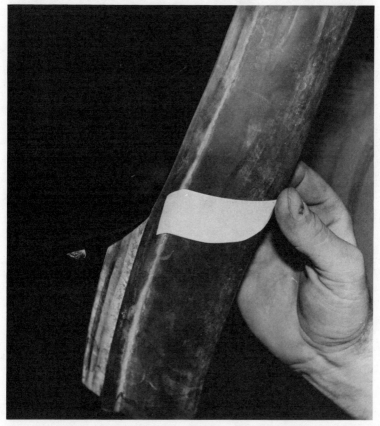

Fig. 19-4. You should have excess lip when you reach the edges of the wheel opening. Place the gummed paper template where you'd like the lip to end.

Fig. 19-5. Trim along the template. This will give all four corners the same smooth curve.

Fig. 19-6. The finished work. Tire lips can make the van legal with large wheels. They also keep the sides of the van cleaner and look sporty.

Fig. 19-7. For extra wide wheels and tires, mud flare units (by Imaginary Glass) are available. A little pinstriping adds flair to the flare.

markets fiberglass running board units designed to coordinate with their flare package (Fig. 19-9). They are sturdily secured to the van by steel brackets that mount to the van's superstructure underneath. This strengthens the boards, too. Secured at each end to the flares themselves, the overall flare/running board setup is both decorative and functional.

Gaining in popularity are the aluminum Road Runners—sturdy, everlasting running boards that do not rust. They mount securely to the inner rocker panels (with brackets) and to inside front and rear wheel wells with heavy bolts. The new aluminum step boards are manufactured by A & E Systems, Santa Ana, California and Doug Thorley (the header and pipe people), Los Angeles, California. These or similar equivalents may be found at the better van

Fig. 19-8. Flares may be molded in to achieve a better part-of-the-van look. The above average do-it-yourselfer may do the work or hire a good body shop.

or RV shop, because they are fast selling items (Fig. 19-10).

GRILLE CONVERSIONS

Grille conversion kits are also gaining popularity and with good

Fig. 19-9. Customized fiberglass running boards on the Badger "Star Bus" (by Imaginary Glass).

Fig. 19-10. The currently very popular aluminum running boards are very much in demand for recreational-type customs.

Fig. 19-11. Stull Industries markets an excellent selection of tube grilles. Here, a custom installation utilizing a Stull Ford Grille and PVT "Square Pak" headlamp units.

Fig. 19-12. Again, Stull shows us how the front end of the Chevy can be affected by tubular conversion. Stock Chevy lighting is retained; center grillework is cut out to accommodate the Stull unit.

reason. They can transform the stock front end into a customized entity, from mild to wild (Fig. 19-11). Stull Industries, a leading grille kit producer, makes a series of conversions for '75 to '82 Fords, '70 to '82 Chevys and GMCs, and '70 to '82 Dodges. These

Fig. 19-13. A home custom fabrication with double quad light setup. This is most distinctive and effective.

Fig. 19-14. PVT Van Trekk grille in Dodge van. This attractive grille sports distinctive space age design that really dresses up any front end.

use the standard grille frames and require minimal cutting and modification (Fig. 19-12). In addition to tubular chromed grille sections, Stull can provide rectangular bulb kits with universal moun-

Fig. 19-15. Another popular PVT Van Trekk grille, but for the Ford, utilizing stock Ford marker lights mounted by the custom quad headlights. Van Trekks are also available for Chevy and GMC vans.

Fig. 19-16. A redwood strip grille adds a distinctive, nautical flavor to this Dodge van.

ting plates, bezels, and necessary conversion hardware. The Stull kits are the easiest to mount. They are very popular among do-it-yourselfers (Fig. 19-13).

PVT Plastics, another custom grille manufacturer, offers two distinctive grille kits that are totally unique. One is the ultramodern, chromed, "Van Trekk" grille featuring four rectangular headlights and blacked-out grill screens. Their second grille is the satin black "Light Rider," with a central acrylic bar illuminated in conjunction with the driving lights. The quad-headlight package included with the "Light Rider" may be purchased separately for customizers who wish to modify their grilles or add quad-lighting (Fig. 19-14).The PVT products are well made and designed. Although some cutting and reconstruction of the stock front end is needed to mount the components, the installation is within the realm of the do-it-yourselfer willing to exercise care and patience. All grille kits available from today's manufacturers may be installed with common household or automotive tools (Fig. 19-15).

Grille kits must be obtained from van shops on special order in most cases because very few van shops stock them in quantity. Year and make of your vehicle must be specified (Fig. 19-16).

SOURCES AND MANUFACTURERS
Flares
Dura Flare-Automotive Accessories Unlimited
2606 Woodland
Anaheim, CA 92801

Imaginary Glass
5417 E. La Palma
Anaheim, CA 92807

Chief Manufacturing Co.
737 Clearlake Road
Cocoa, FL 32922

Running Boards
Imaginary Glass
5417 E. La Palma
Anaheim, CA 92807

Doug Thorley
7403 Telegraph Road
Los Angeles, CA 90040

A & E Systems
1101 S. Linwood Avenue
Santa Ana, CA 92705

Grilles

Stull Industries
7306 Melrose Street
Buena Park, CA 90040

PVT Plastics Corp.
300 Richardson Street
Brooklyn, New York, NY 11222

Chapter 20

Wheels and Tires

Custom wheels are to a van what fine jewelry is to a well-dressed lady. You can do without them, but what a decorative finishing touch they add—like icing on a cake.

CUSTOM WHEELS

Custom wheels first came into being in the mid to late forties when the hot rod set began chroming and modifying stock wheels for custom vehicles. Today, the custom or generically termed "mag" wheel, is a big-selling, sought-after item stocked and promoted by auto specialty supply houses, car dealers, tire centers, and van shops.

Referred to primarily as "mags" (for magnesium), specialized custom wheels are really composed of either steel, aluminum alloy, or a composite of metals. They may be chromed, polished, or anodized. Usually they are lighter in weight than O.E.M. counterparts. The better quality mags are usually truer or rounder than stock issues.

Mainly designed for customs, rods, and competition cars, custom wheels are used on everyday vehicles to enhance the overall appearance. These stylish offerings are so popular that car manufacturers frequently try to emulate them. On vans they provide a finishing touch that complements the design and decor on the van's outer face. When choosing wheels or wheel/tire combinations, van owners usually choose wider wheels and tires to upgrade the handl-

Racer II
(courtesy Rocket Industries)

Racer II full option
(courtesy Rocket Industries)

Fig. 20-1. Wire wheels best suit luxury and sports cars. One some vans, however, they can look choice. These two hail from Rocket Industries.

ing and tractability of the van, while also enhancing the outer decor.

New wheel designs come out every year (Fig. 20-1). Some older patterns still remain, surviving fads and trends to achieve the status of "classics." Classic-types include the traditional wide spoke mag, aluminum slot, and wire wheel. The traditional "Street Spokers," such as the Cragar S/S, Keystone Classic, Rocket Stage I, E-T Diamond Spoke, and Western Super Spoke, are solidly entrenched favorites in the van sales market (Fig. 20-2). Aluminum slot mags have been accepted, but not as widely. They were popular when custom vans were in the embryo stages, but with heavy competition and new designs they have fallen from grace (Fig. 20-3). Smooth and dish mags may be found occasionally on vans, but their solid popularity lies with the performance crowd. A new look exhibited and promoted by Western Wheels is the vaned or turbine design. This has really taken hold in vanning circles. Novel, attractive, and well suited to van decor, these turbine type wheels are manufactured by Western, E-T, and Rocket, all of whom market various patterns based on the sample principle (Fig. 20-4).

Wheel selection should be based mainly on individual taste, but the van's outer existing decor should be considered also. The style of wheel chosen should work with and enhance the outer facade, not overshadow or fight it. For example, wire wheels are by themselves a beauty to behold, but are rarely applicable to vans. Wire wheels were primarily designed with sports and luxury cars

S/S Super Sport (courtesy Cragar Industries)

Super Sabre (courtesy Superior Industries International)

Fig. 20-2. The traditional "Street Spokers" go back a few years but still enjoy wide popularity among the custom van set.

Stage I (courtesy Rocket Industries)

Diamond Spoke (courtesy ET Division—Kelsey Hayes Co.)

Black Spoke (courtesy ET Division-Kelsey Hayes Co.)

Raider (courtesy Keystone Products)

Fig. 20-2. (Continued from page 193.)

194

Superlug (courtesy Superior Industries International)

ET IV (courtesy ET Division—Kelsey Hayes Co.)

Fig. 20-3. Another standard through the years, the slotted aluminum mag. It is not as popular as it once was. here these are two current offerings.

Cyclone RV (courtesy Western Wheel Division, Rockwell Int'l).

Tornado I
(courtesy Rocket Industries)

FWD Tornado I
(courtesy Rocket Industries)

Fig. 20-4. The very popular new "turbine" look as presented by two manufacturers. It is currently very popular in vanning circles.

in mind and serve best when applied in those specific situations (Fig. 20-5). The newest favorites for the vanning crowd are shown in Figs. 20-6 through 20-9.

The major factor to consider when selecting custom wheels is

Dynamo I (courtesy Superior Industries International)

Bullet (courtesy Western Wheel Division, Rockwell Int'l).

Fig. 20-5. An array of dynamic new styles have arrived for custom van buffs. Here are a few from Western, Superior, ET, and Rocket.

Dakota 92 Series (courtesy Superior Industries International)

The Magnus (courtesy Superior Industries International)

Fig. 20-5. (Continued from page 197.)

Kelstar (courtesy ET Division—Kelsey Hayes Co.)

Gunite Mag (courtesy ET Division—Kelsey Hayes Co.)

Radial Spoke (courtesy ET Division—Kelsey Hayes Co.)

199

Vectron
(courtesy Rocket Industries)

Starwood
(courtesy Rocket Industries)

Fig. 20-5. (Continued from page 199.)

proper fit. You must relate the wheel to the offset capabilities of the van wheel drums, and you must consider wheel well and frame clearances.

Offset is the distance from the centerline of the wheel to the bolt plate and is determined by measurement from the centerline. All wheels have an offset (Fig. 20-10). It can be zero (when back of bolt pattern plate is on the rim centerline), positive, or negative. In negative offset, the back of the bolt pattern plate is toward the drum side of the wheel. *Negative offset* allows the wheel to extend further toward the street side of the wheel well. This serves to increase track. Wheels with radical negative offset will extend beyond the sides of the van. This problem can easily be remedied by adding fender flares, which are readily available van accessories. *Positive offset* occurs when the bolt pattern plate is toward the street side of the wheel. With this configuration the centerline of the rim extends further into the wheel well, which serves to decrease track. Radical or deep positive offset may be harder to remedy than negative offset. If the inside wheel flange extends too far into the wheel well, it may make contact with the van frame or wheel well skin.

Back spacing should be closely and critically checked prior to selecting and buying a wheel. Measure from the back of the bolt

Chrome Sprinter

Black Sprinter

Fig. 20-6. The newest look is the Western Sprinter series available in chrome, gold, black, white, or two-tone configurations (courtesy Western Wheels Division, Rockwell Int'l).

White Sprinter

Gold Sprinter

Fig. 20-6. (Continued from page 201.)

202

Vectron I   Black Vectron I

Startrack   Black Startrack

Fig. 20-7. The Vectron and Startralk series by Rocket Industries offer spacy design in all aluminum or black shaded versions (courtesy Rocket Industries).

pad of the wheel to the back of the rim. To ensure proper fit, it is wise to install the wheel without a tire to further check clearance because spring clips, drum rivets, or drum balancing weights may also interfere with mounting calculations. It goes without saying that the proper mounting bolt pattern must be chosen or the wheel cannot be attached to the drum.

White Tracker (courtesy Western Wheel Division, Rockwell)

Nomad (courtesy Cragar Industries)

Fig. 20-8. Let's not forget the all white, punched steel wheels. These are great for four-wheel drive and off-road van versions.

Superstar I (courtesy Superior Industries International)

White Trailbuster (courtesy Rocket Industries)

Fig. 20-8. White Trailbuster (courtesy Rocket Industries).

205

Fig. 20-9. The "Smoothie," from Rocket, is an oldie but goodie. It is very uncommon on vans, but attractive when used in the proper situation.

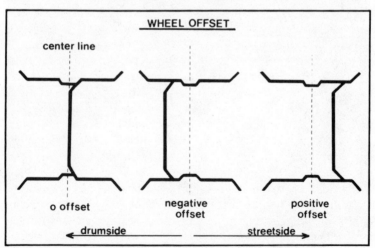

Fig. 20-10. Changing wheels from stock to custom can change the offset of the wheels. This must be corrected for proper tractability.

TIRES

Once the wheel problem is solved, consideration must be given to tire selection. Close attention must be paid to the width of the tire between the wheel rim circumference and the tire tread to prevent radial runout problems. *Radial runout* is the up and down motion of the wheel and tire as it rotates. Too high a tire and too much radial runout may cause a tire to hit the inside of the wheel well. Bumpy road conditions can also affect the up and down travel of the wheel and allowances must be made.

Lateral runout is another idiosyncracy to be considered. This is the side-to-side motion of the wheel as it rotates. Too wide a tire/wheel combination up front may also inhibit steering, so careful study must apply here, too. If all the aforementioned data seems confusing, put your trust in a wheel, tire, or van dealer who is familiar with these problems and calculations and can best advise you in wheel and tire selection.

There is not much actual difference between tires, usually just their performance characteristics (Fig. 20-11). In some cases tire selection is governed by price: "How good a tire can I get?" and "How little can I pay? What's on sale?" When going for replacement tires the van owner, in virtually all instances, will choose a wider or "fat" tire. This must be mounted on a wider than stock rim.

There are no set rules pertaining to aesthetics in tires; they basically all look alike. The main factors to consider are handling and tracking capabilities while the van is in motion. The primary rule is: don't mix different kinds of tires on a van if possible. It doesn't look good and can be dangerous, too.

Whenever feasible, use the same type of tires on all four wheels—all radials or all bias ply. Intermixing the two is not advisable because they exhibit different performance characteristics. If it becomes necessary to utilize both (because of economics, budget, availability, etc.), never mount a radial opposite a bias ply (on a common axle). If you have two of each kind, you can mount the bias ply up front, the radials in back. Unfortunately this does not work as well vice versa because of the different *slip angles* of the two tire types. The slip angle is the variance between the steering of the driver and the actual travel of the van. Contrasting slip angles encountered by unequal front and back tires will cause the van to understeer or oversteer. Front tires with a slip angle greater than that of the rear tires will cause the van to understeer. The van will turn reluctantly so that the driver must jockey the van into

Pro-Trac 70

High Roller

High Roller

Fig. 20-11. Probably the best tires available for vans are the Pro-Trac line. Excellent all-weather tires, they perform better than most tires under wet road conditions (courtesy Pro-Trac Tire Co., Inc.).

208

Pro-Trac 60

Pro-Trac Optimum

R/P Radial

Eagle ST

Eagle NCT

Eagle GT

F32 All Winter Radial

Fig. 20-12. Goodyear offers several fine tires for custom vans (courtesy Goodyear Tire and Rubber Co.).

the turn. The van will, however, remain under the driver's control if the understeer is not excessive. When the rear tires have a greater slip angle than the front tires, oversteer will occur. This causes the van to turn on a tighter radius than may be desired. This overtight turn situation must be corrected by the driver's steering out of the curve.

After tires are mounted and broken in, they should be cared for at regular intervals. Check tire pressures weekly. Check for abnormal wear: feather edging, scalloping, bald spots, uneven tread

Safari A-T

Safari R-T

Safari RVR

Fig. 20-13. Seven Kelly tires that do well on any van (courtesy Kelly-Springfield Tire Co.).

211

Super Charger

Wide Super Charger

Wide Super Charger

Super Charger

Fig. 20-13. (Continued from page 211.)

212

wear, or cracked treads. Rotate the tires at reasonable intervals. When tire walls become dirty, treat them with Armor-All, which is a great tire rejuvenator, cleaner, and protectant.

When choosing wheels and tires, analyze all the aforementioned prerequisites and apply them to your particular situation. Also consider the vendor's recommendations and trust to his experience and expertise. See Figs. 20-12 through 20-14.

To aid you in wheel and tire selection, the following suppliers have been listed. They may be contacted by mail and will readily forward desired information and brochures on their current offerings.

WHEEL MANUFACTURERS

E-T Division—Kelsey Hayes Co.
Benicia Industrial Park
Benicia, CA 94510

Western Wheel Division—Rockwell Int'l.
6951 Walker Street
La Palma, CA 90623

Rocket Industries
9935 Beverly Boulevard
Pico Rivera, CA 90660

Keystone Products Inc.
1333 South Bon View Avenue
Ontario, CA 91761

Superior Industries
7800 Woodley Avenue
Van Nuys, CA 91406

TIRE MANUFACTURERS

Armstrong Rubber Co.
500 Sargent Drive
New Haven, CT 06507

B.F. Goodrich Co.
500 South Main Street
Akron, OH 44317

Radial ATX

Super Sports

S/S Radial

Fig. 20-14. A collection of Firestone tires for vans (courtesy Firestone Tire and Rubber Co.).

HPR Radial

Super Sports, wide

S/S Radial

215

Firestone Tire and Rubber Co.
1200 Firestone Parkway
Akron, OH 44317

Goodyear Tire and Rubber Co.
1144 East Market Street
Akron, OH 44316

Pro-Trac Tire Co.
425 North Robertson Boulevard
Los Angeles, CA 90048

Dayton Tire and Rubber Co.
Box 1026
Dayton, OH 45401

Dunlop Tire and Rubber Co.
Box 1109
Buffalo, NY 14240

Kelly-Springfield Tire Co.
P.O. Box 300
Cumberland, MD 21502

Chapter 21

Painting the Van

The crowning glory of the customized van is the exterior paint job. It is the first item to catch the eye on the road, in a show, or when the vehicle is at rest in a public parking space. A well-executed paint job will draw and hold spectator interest while providing the owner with a unique expression of his individuality. The aesthetic approach can be mild or wild, depending on individual taste, preference, and budget limitations. At one time murals or combined murals and graphics were the accepted formula for van painting. Today, exterior design aesthetics have given way to simple yet tasteful graphic renderings more economical to produce and easier to repair and match when scratched or mutilated in collisions (Fig. 21-1).

If you intend to farm out your van to an approved custom painter, be prepared to spend money. Good design and quality paint do not come cheap. If you care to do it yourself (and you can if you exercise patience and care), then read on. This chapter is devoted to the staunch do-it-yourself van enthusiast who wishes to express himself by creating an exterior that will be part of him both in expression and execution.

We will begin with the basis, explaining paint systems, materials, and equipment. Then we'll move on to more specialized artistic approaches, distinctive yet simple enough for even the neophyte to tackle, provided he follows instructions closely. We will illustrate and explain in detail mural and graphic rendering,

Fig. 21-1. One approach to graphics and shading.

with simplified approaches within the realm of the average layman (Fig. 21-2).

There are a few accepted and proven methods for automotive surface refinishing that have become the refinishing basis in painting today. The choice left to the individual is usually based on specified product availability, product quality and durability, cost, time factors involved in application, and condition of the under-surface to be recoated. Complete removal of old or factory paint may also play a great part in the selection of recoat mediums because some paints lend themselves better to recoating over certain materials than others. If painting over an unpainted surface (aluminum, steel, fiberglass, ABS plastic), it is best to check if the automotive refinishing product you've chosen will work on that surface. Checking with the paint manufacturers and browsing through the instructive repaint manuals will help you select materials for proper refinish/surface compatibility.

Refinishing systems or paints for automotive use are comprised of three categories or types, each one differing from the other in various degrees and characteristics. When choosing a system, follow through with the complete, one-brand system of paints and their equivalent thinners and additives. Mismatching will cause deviations and, in some instances, major catastrophic reactions. Most pros chose to use one manufacturer's brand throughout, both the paint of a specific manufacturer and the solvents manufactured

Fig. 21-2. Two more graphic approaches showing how the design work coordinates with the windows.

by the same. Intermixing of brand names or generic substitution is not recommended.

FINISHES

The basic finishes offered to the professional and general public are:

- Synthetic enamel
- Acrylic lacquer
- Acrylic enamel

Synthetic enamels are about the oldest types of auto refinish materials. They require few topcoats to realize a high gloss and don't need polishing or buffing. These enamels are economical in price, in relation to lacquers and acrylic enamels, and readily available. Synthetic enamels are easy to apply because they will easily adhere to practically all surfaces. They also require only minimal surface preparation. Their popularity has diminished greatly in recent years because they take a long time to dry and cure and must be applied carefully. They are prone to sagging and running when sprayed on too heavily. Because synthetic enamels dry so slowly, they are also inclined to pick up dust from the air, which tends to blemish the surface. This medium is definitely not recommended for the backyard or garage painter; synthetic enamels are best applied in spray booths under controlled dust conditions.

Acrylic lacquers are one of the main standbys. They are relatively easy to apply due to their quick-dry characteristics. Acrylic lacquer finishes are fairly durable and weather resistant and have excellent color and gloss retention. Color must be built up gradually with consecutive coats that dry quickly to allow rapid application for proper coverage. Because weather conditions, heat, and humidity can adversely affect the application and finish, good working knowledge of the various thinners and reducers required for acrylic lacquers is mandatory for obtaining optimum results under adverse climatic conditions. To obtain maximum luster, acrylic lacquers should be buffed and compounded. This will guarantee the glass like, flawless finish attributed to acrylic lacquer.

Acrylic enamels (catalyzed acrylic enamels and urethanes) are the newest finishes. They are said to combine the better features of both synthetic enamels and acrylic lacquers. Acrylic enamels are easy to apply, drying much quicker than synthetic enamels, but not as rapidly as acrylic lacquers. Acrylic enamel films will not run or sag as easily as synthetic enamel, but they will dry to an above-average gloss that offers maximum durability and protection. Some quick-dry acrylic enamels may be recoated or two-toned after a six-hour drying period, particularly if a hardening or catalyzing additive has been added. Urethane and additive hardeners (catalysts) increase the durability and gloss of the acrylic enamels for which they are produced. The hardeners make the finish highly resistant to stone chips, scratches, and many chemical elements. The catalyst or hardener broadens the advantage scope of the acrylic enamel solution. The mirror finish that results from catalyzed acrylic enamel will retain its gloss and color longer and remains tougher than either synthetic or conventional acrylic enamel. The hardener additive also leaves the finish less sensitive for quick recoating if necessary.

THINNERS AND THEIR APPLICATION

Thinners and solvents play a major role in preparing paint to thinning it so that it may be properly sprayed or atomized within the spray gun or spraying tool. There are thinners for synthetic resin base products, acrylic enamels and urethanes, and acrylic lacquers. As a rule, they are not interchangeable and should be used only with the medium for which they were formulated. Optimum results are achieved when a thinner balanced for its proper paint medium is used to dissolve the ingredient of each particular medium, allowing it to flow out to its maximum smoothness and effectiveness.

Alkyd Enamel Reducers

Alkyd enamels cover well with no excessive reduction necessary if properly applied. Many people err in trying to apply too heavy a coat. An overly thick film of enamel is not necessarily more durable. A normally applied film thickness will, in most cases, hold up better and may be less prone to running and sagging. Running and sagging may also occur if the solution to be sprayed is overly thinned. The proper reduction ratio for alkyd enamels is 33 1/3 percent—one part reducer to three parts enamel. This ratio makes an ideal viscosity for spraying.

When spraying this solution through a standard syphon production gun, the air pressure at the gun should be maintained between 50 to 65 pounds for a proper flow out with no sags or excessive film thickness. Three reducer solutions may be obtained for use with alkyd enamels. One is the *standard all-around* or *all-weather reducer,* which sets up the paint quickly and inhibits runs while permitting proper flow out. A *cold-shop reducer* may be more applicable for temperature conditions under 60 degrees, where the faster drying action may be advantageous. A *hot-weather reducer* is seldom used, but in high heat conditions it may be required. Hot-weather reducers also serve as retarders in cases where an all-weather reducer is not adequate to allow the paint to flow out evenly.

Acrylic Enamel Reducers

Acrylic enamels are generally easy to apply, fast drying, and exceedingly more durable than conventional enamels and acrylic lacquers. Care similar to that followed in spraying alkyd enamels should be exercised to realize a flawless finish. Generally, the blend ratio of one part reducer to two parts paint (or 50 percent reduction) is the proper paint thinner formulation. Effective spray pressure at the gun should be between 50 and 60 pounds. Because air pressure may critically affect the final finish with acrylic enamels, experiment between these limits to obtain the right paint and application consistency combination.

Most manufacturers supply three types of acrylic enamel reducers. A *low temperature reducer* is advised for subnormal shop temperatures (below 75 degrees). An *all-around* or *medium speed reducer* will work well for normal shop temperatures between 70 degrees and 85 degrees. A *slow dry enamel reducer* is recommended for exceedingly warm temperatures and highly humid conditions. Slow dry acrylic enamel thinners are seldom used except in situations where a retardant action is required either because of high temperature or to gain better flow out.

Acrylic Lacquer Thinners

Because acrylic lacquers are so fast drying, they are more sensitive to temperature and weather reactions that may cause deviations affecting color, gloss, and flow out. If temperature conditions are not compensated for, problems such as chalking or blushing, sand scratch swelling, poor adhesion, and poor color matching may occur. All acrylic lacquer manufacturers offer three basic grades of thinner: fast, medium, and slow-drying. There are also retarders that, when added to conventional thinners, slow down the drying time to increase the gloss factor, eliminate blushing, and improve flow out to minimize orange peel and achieve smoother paint film surface.

Fast-dry or *nonpenetrating thinners* are ideal for spot repair painting, primer dilution, and cold weather application. Due to the limited penetrating quality, a fast-dry thinner is highly recommended for application of a sensitive surface that may react to a hotter or slow drying penetrating thinner. Because nonpenetrating type thinners evaporate so quickly, they may promote poor adhesion. They also may cause blushing particularly when used in a high heat or humid atmosphere. The blushing or chalking (denoted by a whitish dull cast) is caused by fast evaporation, which causes moisture to be trapped within the film. The blushing syndrome may be prevented if it occurs by moving up to a slower drying thinner or adding retarder to the quick drying solvent. The fast evaporation characteristic of the nonpenetrating thinner can also contribute to orange peeling. This may have to be corrected by sanding or retarding the solvent solution.

All-purpose or *medium speed thinners* are great for undercoats, overcoats, and general shop use. They are moderately priced and, under well-balanced atmospheric and temperature conditions, will provide adequate flow out and moderate to good gloss. If necessary, all-purpose thinners may have retarder added to them to slow down drying time and solvent evaporation to gain higher gloss and better flow out.

Slow drying thinners, usually considered the highest grade thinners (and also the most expensive), are often referred to as "high boil" thinners because they are heavy in solvent strength and evaporate slowly. The slow drying characteristic sets them apart from general all-purpose thinners, which are weak in solvent strength and tend to evaporate more rapidly. Slow-dry thinners are excellent for fault free color coating, provide optimum film flow out, and are a body shop mainstay where high heat and humidity conditions are prevalent. Slow-dry thinners do much to inhibit orange peel and blushing.

Choice of thinners is sometimes critical and each of their characteristics should be studied and applied properly. Thinners must dissolve and reduce paint while holding all the ingredients in proper suspension. It must also evaporate to leave the film smooth but at a speed that will not cause adverse reactions or affect the adhesion or durability of the dried film.

Retarder is another solvent medium used in conjunction with or added to any of the aforementioned thinners either to improve flow, minimize orange peel, or provide high resistance to blushing. The addition of retarder may also be necessary or mandatory for adjusting the thinner to allow it to work properly in high temperatures or in humid weather.

When in doubt about solvent reduction and mixing, refer to the paint label. It will spell out the requirements of a proper spraying solution and proper reduction percentage. The following list will help convert the percentages to the actual proportion of paint and thinner.

25 percent	=	one part thinner to four parts paint
33 percent	=	one part thinner to three parts paint
50 percent	=	one part thinner to two parts paint
100 percent	=	one part thinner to one part paint
125 percent	=	five parts thinner to four parts paint
150 percent	=	three parts thinner to two parts paint
200 percent	=	two parts thinner to one part paint

EQUIPMENT

Spray equipment is necessary and is actually the only feasible means of applying paint to automobiles and various automotive parts. There are several types of spraying utensils for van work, the choice made according to specific application purposes.

The production gun is the most common and necessary spray tool. Several production spray guns are marketed and available in all auto paint refinishing shops. The most well-known and accepted quality brands names are DeVilbiss, Sharpe, Binks, Rodac, and Marson. Sears also markets a few production guns, budget priced, and in some cases, equivalent in quality to the more expensive brand name offerings.

The siphon-type spray gun is generally considered the body shop mainstay. It is used in conjunction with a spray compressor that provides air to power the gun fluid atomization. In the siphon-type gun, the trigger acts as the control for the air and fluid and controls the intermixing of both air and paint (atomization). To obtain a proper working consistency, it is necessary to properly mix paint to thinner ratios. (The proper mixing and metering is covered in detail in the paints and thinners segment.) To work efficiently and properly, the production gun must be well maintained, which usually means disassembled, cleaned, and flushed at frequent intervals or after use. The air and fluid passages should be kept free of paint buildup. The air valve stem, fluid needle packing, and various working parts should be kept lubricated as recommended in the manufacturer's instruction sheet. The air vent opening in the spray cup cap should always be kept free from paint blockage, or erratic spraying will take place.

The spray gun is relatively simple to operate, even for the novice. The trigger is simply pulled back; the further back it is pulled, the greater the fluid (paint) emitted. Proper fluid, air, and fan spray settings are set by two external primed knobs that governs the width of the spray or "fan." Turning the knob all the way clockwise will concentrate the patter into a small circle, a setting ideal for small area work. Turning this screw to the left (counterclockwise) elongates the pattern into an oval. At maximum "out" setting, the widest spray coverage is achieved.

The lower knob controls the amount of fluid by allowing the fluid needle to be retracted and set by revolving the knob in and out. The fluid needle is usually set to emit larger amounts of fluid as the spray pattern setting is widened. As fan spray setting is increased, more fluid must be emitted to obtain proper coverage over wider areas.

Spray Gun Operation

Even though spray gun manipulation is not difficult and within the realm of the average layman, the beginner should develop his technique up to the point where he will be able to lay down a spray coating efficiently and flawlessly. This requires constant practice, both with gun and with paint and thinner mixing ratios. The amount of paint applied to fully cover a surface will depend on the number of coats applied, distance form gun to the surface, and fluid reduction. This all requires a good operation technique.

In operation, the spray gun will perform best at a distance of about 10 to 12 inches away from the surface to be painted. At shorter distances film rippling, due to air pressure or a buildup of paint, which may tend to sag and run, may result. If the distance is greater than a foot or so, dry film surfaces will cause orange peel. As the paint is being applied, the gun should always be held parallel to the surface at a constantly equal distance from the start to the finish of the stroke. If the gun is tilted or the nozzle angled so that the fan pattern is not uniform as in a parallel stroke, or the gun is swinging in an arc toward the surface, the paint will go on wetter where the spray is closer or drier where the fan is further away. Always overlap one spray stroke with the consecutive one by about 50 percent to achieve a uniform blend of tone or color. The central, heavy fluid wielding part of the spray fan should be directed at the lower edge of the previous stroke. If all these recommendations are followed, a uniform paint film results.

The Touch-Up Gun

The touch-up or jamb gun is the smaller counterpart of the production gun. Smaller in size and volumetric paint content, the touch-up gun is ideal for small area coverage and in tight areas where production guns would create an overspray problem. The touch-up gun is ideal for small spot painting situations and particularly for painting inside doorjamb areas because the spray can be controlled and concentrated without any danger of paint damage to adjacent interior areas.

The leading touch-up guns in widespread use today are the Badger 400, Binks 15, and DeVilbiss EGA. All are easily hand-held and triggered by an upper lever manipulated by the forefinger. The

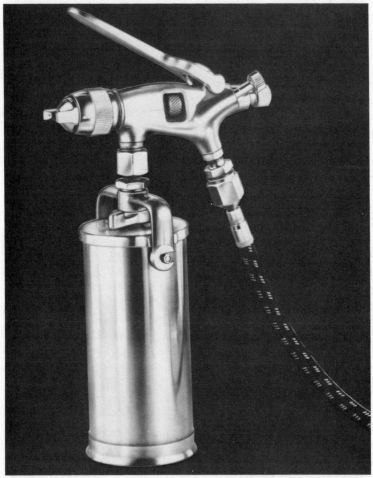

Fig. 21-3. The Badger 400 detail gun. Ideal for detailing murals and fine edge shading.

Binks 15 comes in a right-hand or left-hand control version. The DeVilbiss touch-up gun can be used right or left-handed. The new Badger 400 has a flip-over control lever than can be adjusted to operate in a left-hand or right hand mode (Fig. 21-3). Very similar to the production gun in adjustment, the touch-up guns have a fan spray adjustment and a fluid needle setting adjustment. In the DeVilbiss and Badger, the thumbscrew adjustments are at the rear. The Binks 15 has its fan spray control at the forward part of the gun directly behind the air cap.

Touch-up guns have interchangeable air caps and needles for regular or extra fine work. The extra fine configuration makes the touch-up gun a close second to the airbrush for medium tonal rendering and artwork. Some muralists work with touch-up guns for fine painting, particularly edge shading and border toning when painting graphics on motorcycles, cars, and vans. A good touch-up gun is a welcome and handy addition to the spray equipment roster. Many professionals would be lost without one for custom work. The touch-up gun bridges the gap between production gun and airbrush very well. With their varied replaceable air needles and nozzles, the touch-up guns can provide spray width pattern sizes from 1/4-inch to a little over 3 inches depending on the nozzles and needles used.

The Airbrush

The airbrush is the most refined of the spray guns—the artist's utensil, so to speak. Airbrushes were primarily designed for the commercial art and photographic field. With the advent of murals on custom cars and vans, the airbrush was quickly adopted by custom painters because such fine rendering and drawing could be achieved with this extra fine minispray tool. A number of airbrushes are available at better art stores. Some are for extra fine line rendering and photographic retouching, while others, more adaptable to custom van work, will capably handle the quick drying and highly coagulent automotive lacquers and "trick" custom paints. The airbrushes best suited to automotive custom painting and muralization are the Paasche VL5, the Thayer & Chandler E, Thayer & Chandler C, the Badger 150, and the Badger 200.

There are two types of airbrushes—single action or double action. The single-action airbrush is an internal mix unit that releases air and paint in an atomized or "spray" state as the trigger button is depressed. The fan spray width and paint volume emitted is controlled and regulated by a separate knob, usually located at the rear of such units as the Thayer & Chandler and Badger brushes. Fan spray width and paint volume can also be controlled by revolving a spray control cone, which is an integral part of the air and paint nozzle of such models as Paasche single action, Binks Wren, or Badger 350.

In the double-action airbrush the control button acts as both a paint emission lever and a spray width regulator on a coordinated basis. Depressing the button or lever allows pure air to flow. As the depressed button is pulled back in a sliding action (the button is linked to the paint flow needle), the needle is retracted and paint is allowed to flow through the spray nozzle. The more the needle is retracted, the more the paint flow and the larger a spray width achieved.

Veteran airbrush painters prefer the versatility of the double-action airbrush, while beginners and neophytes adapt more easily to the easily controlled single-action airbrushes. Though many airbrushes are marketed, certain types lend themselves better to spraying automotive type lacquers with trouble-free results and minimal clogging. The models most frequently used and recommended are the Binks Wren, Badger 150 HD, Badger 200 HD, Paasche VL, Paasche H3, Thayer & Chandler Model C, and Thayer & Chandler Model E.

AIRBRUSHING LACQUERS

The refined pigments and binders of automotive lacquers make them ideal for mural rendering or graphic design enhancement. Because the needle openings and spray orifices of all airbrushes are thin and narrow, they are readily prone to blocking and clogging as lacquers are fast drying and coagulative liquids. To work well in conjunction with airbrushes, lacquers must be thinned out to a greater degree. A greater proportion of thinner to paint ratio must be used for proper airbrush manipulation and rendering. A good starting point or mixing ratio is four to one—four parts thinner to one part paint. In instances where delicate detailing is required or the airbrush tip is extremely narrow, a five to one ratio (five parts thinner to one part paint) may be required. For larger, heavy-duty airbrushes a three to one (three parts thinner to one part paint) ratio is feasible. To keep the airbrush working properly and to inhibit spitting or clogging while in use, frequent flushing with straight thinner is highly recommended. Medium to fast drying thinners are also recommended when using airbrushes for mural detailing or in conjunction with stencils. To learn how to manipulate the airbrush and attain expertise in operation, consult the instruction manual supplied with the airbrush, or purchase one of the many airbrush instruction manuals that cover airbrush techniques.

MASKING AND TAPING

Masking, taping, and design masking are all critically important regarding repaint, spot touch, or custom paint jobs. Proper and efficient masking techniques should always be used to achieve a perfect paint job with clean, sharp-edge design rendering.

Many basic grades of masking tapes are available to the automotive trade. When looking for a tape, it is strongly suggested that the better grades of tape be used regardless of their higher price. Most discriminating custom finishers rely heavily on automotive grade 3M Scotch masking tapes, which are considered the best quality. These masking tapes (a paper-crepe type) come in varied sizes from 1/8 inch up to 3 inches in width. The thinner widths will conform to tighter, smaller curves. This makes them ideal for design masking or in tight areas. The thinner the tape, the smaller a curve or radius it will negotiate. The extra wide tape (3 inches) is used for filling in large areas quickly and efficiently and will not readily curve. This makes it feasible only for large gap coverage. The most common sizes used in painting and refinishing are the 1/2-inch to 2-inch tapes. The extra thin tapes such as 1/8 and 1/4 inch are basically used in design or custom applications.

As important as tape is masking paper, another paint shop staple. Masking paper comes in large rolls in sizes from 3 inches up to 24 inches. Masking paper rolls are primarily designed for use in special dispensers. They dispense the paper and tape at the same time. The tape adheres to the paper edge automatically as the paper is pulled from the dispenser. If you are undertaking small or infrequent jobs, the paper and tape may be applied manually with equally ideal, if slower, results. One-inch or 3/4-inch masking tape is most commonly chosen for use with masking paper. The areas that must be masked off are the windows and parts that are impossible or difficult to remove such as the chrome strips, medallions, and emblems.

Design masking covers cover paneling, enhancement of body lines, and striping or similar decor usually limited in factory paint jobs but used extensively in custom painting. To lay out or duplicate a factory stripe or add a custom design motif, 1/8-inch tape is usually used to lay out the design pattern outline. The outer or peripheral areas are then masked off using paper and masking tape to control overspray or paint leak-through.

A spray mask is another accepted masking medium and is available from many automotive paint specialty shops. Spray mask is used extensively by custom painters and muralists. It is applied in a liquid state with production gun in the same manner that paint is applied. After spray mask has fully dried (about four hours), it takes on a rubbery, transparent appearance and conforms to the surface like a glove. The design or stripes to be painted are then drawn onto the dried film with a magic marker or grease pencil. The area to be painted is cut out with an X-Acto knife or razor blade using a pressure sufficient to cut into the masking film, but not heavy enough to cut into the undersurface paint film. The cut portion is then peeled off leaving a tight outline film that acts as an excellent and efficient mask.

Spray mask is water based and very viscous in nature. It may be used in its thick state or may be thinned down with water. Because it is so thick in its stock form, you should use a spray gun with a large spray nozzle opening so that the liquid is properly and evenly transferred to the surface to be masked and painted. Spray mask is unparalleled for intricate design masking and custom rendering.

"TRICK" PAINTS

Before getting into some simple but effective custom painting techniques, some of the "trick" custom paint mediums will be described.

Candies

Candies, the most alluring of "trick" paints, are nothing more than basic toners that are translucent in nature. When applied, they do not build up an opaque film—undercoats and undercoatings show through and, in virtually all cases, affect the tonality of the final built-up color. Candies are the most difficult of colors to apply. Usually they are sprayed over a silver or gold metallic ground coat to enhance the overall effect. They can also be laid over opaque colored ground coats, but may shift or change in tonality according to the color used underneath. Candies are not sprayed on like opaque mediums. They are hazed on in *thin*, even, light coats until the desired color or density is achieved. If runs occur or dirt gets into the paint, it will continue to show through the consecutive coats. In most cases if a candy job is ruined either through carelessness or improper manipulation of the spraying tool, it must be removed and painted over.

Painting with candies is not recommended for the novice do-it-yourselfer. One should learn and master the idiosyncrasies of candy paint before attempting a job that may be fruitless if not properly executed. Candy colors are manufactured by the Metal Flake Corporation and Aero-Lac and can be purchased at better automotive paint stores.

Pearls

Pearls, the most exotic of paint finishes, are easily recognizable by their pearllike finishes. Three trick pearl paints are marketed: Pearlescent, Murano, and Eerie-Dess. Pearlescents are semi-transparent, iridescent coatings. Muranos are color varying, diffraction-type coatings. Eerie-Dess is a pearl design medium mainly used in an applique process.

Pearl trick paints are produced mainly by the Metal Flake Corporation, Haverhill, Massachusetts. Pearls are applied in the same fashion as candies, though they are not as translucent. Pearlescent pigment is composed of a tiny fish scale base that, when dried, flashes off its own color.

Semitransparent pearls are generally applied over a base or ground coat that may be of the same or different color to enhance the finished paint job. The most popular paint undercoats for achieving favorable and trick effects with pearls are white, black, and silver. If a solid opaque pearl look is desired, a base coating of a hue similar to the pearlescent hue is advised. Pearlescents should be administered with care in consecutive mist coats with adequate drying time in between. Final coating with clear acrylic lacquer (about four coats) is strongly advised as pearls cannot be directly sanded or buffed without marring the finish.

Murano Pearls

Easily discerned for their refractive or reflective characteristic when viewed at an angle, Muranos are the most translucent of all custom pigment. It almost completely *allows* base color to show through unaffected. Viewed at a direct 90-degree angle, they allow the under base color to show through almost unaffected; when studied at an angle, they radiate a pearly hue of their own. The Murano hues available are gold, silver gold, silver, yellow, green, blue, red, and aqua. They are available in pastelike forms to be mixed with

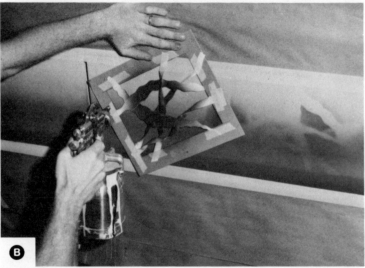

Fig. 21-4. A novel op-art design panel can evolve through the use of a mask (A) constructed according to text. Spray through mask at consecutive intervals (B). Then spray again with the same mask over the panel, this time overlapping previous stencil transfer (C). The finished job is shown in (D).

diluted clear acrylic to form a working solution. Ready-to-use, properly diluted Muranos are marketed by Metal Flake under the trade name of "Flip-Flop." When spraying Muranos or any typical pearl

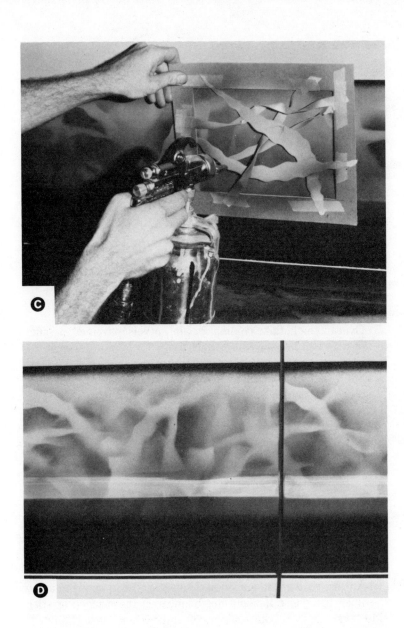

type paint medium, be sure to shake the spray gun frequently to keep the pearl particles well suspended and uniform throughout the working solution.

Eerie-Dess

So-called for the eerie design effects it can produce, Eerie-Dess is a pearl design medium for trick, hand-manipulated use. It is a slow-drying mineral base solution laden with pearl particles and available in blue, red, silver, green, and gold colors. Marketed in premixed, ready-to-use cans, Eerie-Dess is applied in the usual manner. Before Eerie-Dess has dried, it is dabbed and worked over in appliqué fashion to achieve distinctively novel effects.

The still wet sprayed-on file is reworked with pressed-on, then pulled-off wrinkled aluminum foil or Saran Wrap to obtain a crystalized design effect. After design manipulation is finished, the Eerie-Dess is allowed to fully dry for about one half hour, after which it can be overcoated and sealed with about five coats of clear acrylic lacquer. Candies may also be applied over Eerie-Dess coats for heightened or varied color effects.

Metalflake

Overall, thick, flake coating or painting was extremely popular in the fifties and sixties. Its popularity has waned in favor of the more subtle and intriguing candy and pearl finishes, which are not as garish heavy Metalflake coatings. In some scattered instances Metalflake is still applied for partial enhancement in graphic situations. The most popular flakes in use today are the finer Micro Sequin flakes produced by Ditzler that produce heightened metallic finishes as opposed to the overall "nugget" flake effects typical of the fifties and sixties.

In full Metalflake painting, the flakes replace the pigments of ordinary paints and are suspended in a working solution of diluted clear acrylic. The suspended flake solution is sprayed through a standard production gun creating a deep layer of clear paint, saturated with reflecting flake particles. Flakes are usually sprayed over a similarly colored base coat or contrasting color base coats for different color effects.

Air pressure at the gun should not exceed 25 pounds to allow the flake to adhere flat and not bounce off the surface or stick sideways, a problem that may manifest itself when using standard spraying pressures. To keep the flake in constant and proper suspension within the diluted clear solution, the gun should be thoroughly shaken or agitated prior to each spray pass. A good working ratio between flake and clear is about 4 to 5 ounces of flake to 1 quart of clear acrylic.

A color card containing samples of all colors and types of flakes, candies, and pearls may be obtained from: Metal Flake Corp., P.O. Box 950, Haverhill, MA, 01830.

DESIGN MOTIFS

To end this custom painting chapter, we feature two approaches that can be easily and properly affected by even the novice painter. One is a graphic paneling approach, the other a simple mural rendering.

Fig. 21-5. First, a stencil is cut out for the darker gray areas to be rendered in an approved stencil medium.

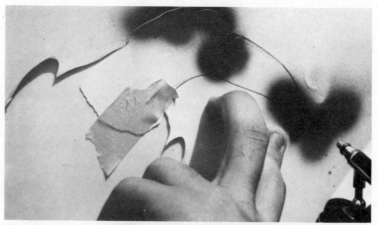

Fig. 21-6. The blacks and grays are toned in with the airbrush.

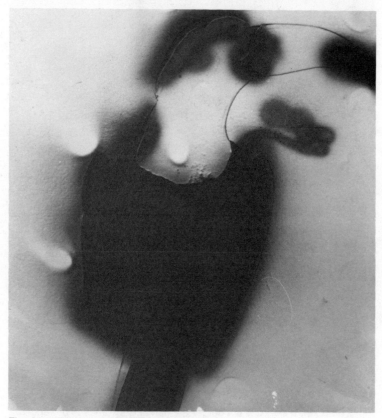

Fig. 21-7. The body is then toned and shaded.

Fig. 21-8. When the stencil is removed, a basic shape remains.

The paneling approach has proved to be most effective, simple, and aesthetically pleasing (Fig. 21-4). To obtain a novel op-art design motif, a mask is constructed consisting of a heavy cardboard frame entwined with strips and shapes as shown. Some of the strips

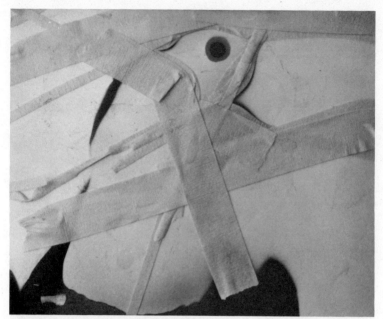

Fig. 21-9. The beak area is masked off.

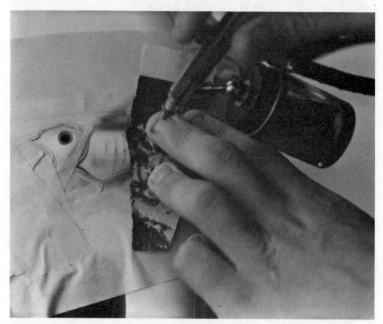

Fig. 21-10. Highlights re added to the beak using a piece of torn paper

238

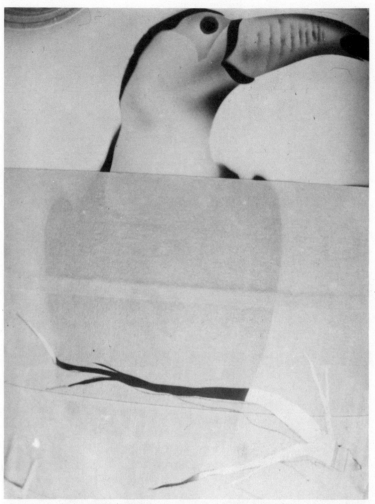

Fig. 21-11. Shadows are added to the face, then masking tape is laid over the lower portion. The outline for the branch is cut out with a razor blade, and the inner portion is peeled off.

are applied flush with the back of the frame, some flush with the front of the frame. Some are twisted before attaching. When the frame is held against the surface of the van, some of the integrated strips will directly contact the surface to be painted while others will be suspended at a short distance from the surface.

When spraying through this mask or stencil, the edges touching the surface will leave sharp edges; the suspended edges will leave soft edges. The combination will create novel effects. Move the

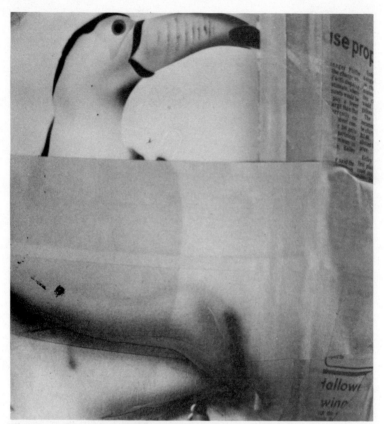

Fig. 21-12. The branch is airbrushed in.

Fig. 21-13. Foliage is stippled on with a brush dipped in acrylic lacquer.

240

stencil along the masked panel area and spray color at chosen intervals. Start with one color, then make passing, consecutive, overlapping designs utilizing contrasting or harmonizing colors. Build up a design and color pattern to suit your own taste. When complete, you will be astonished at the magnificent, eye-catching results.

The mural approach exhibited illustrates the rendering of a bird, a simple undertaking even for the ranking amateur. The step-by-step procedure presented in Figs. 21-5 through 21-14 shows a simple airbrush rendering executed with stencil, airbrush, acrylic lacquer, and some care and patience. Follow the instructions closely and you, too, can make accurate and favorable facsimile of this simple subject. An expanded version of this technique is shown in Figs. 21-15 and 21-16.

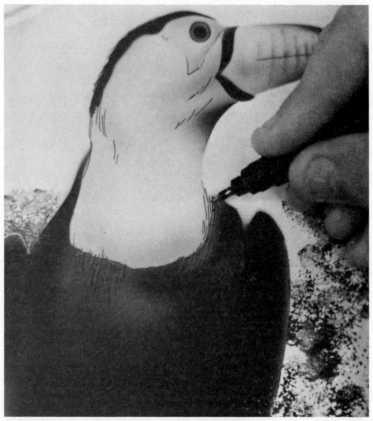

Fig. 21-14. Final detailing is added with a rapidograph pen and india ink. The entire mural is coated with five coats of clear lacquer.

Fig. 21-15. Finished mural using the same technique as described in text for bird but expanded upon (paint and mural by Carl Caiati).

Another simplistic paneling approach is wood graining, very popular today and favored by both custom and recreational van buffs (Figs. 21-17A and 21-17B). Wood grain effects are striking and authentic looking. They are particularly effective when used in panels or integrated with graphics. To achieve the striking grain pattern, a wood grain squeegee is used. The squeegee contains elliptical ridges on its concave surface that produce the grain pattern. Wood graining is so simple that a child can do it.

First, a light brown base coat of acrylic lacquer is applied to the section masked off to be grained. Then a solution or wash is formulated consisting of black acrylic enamel diluted with six parts of enamel reducer. This solution is placed in a spray gun and ap-

Fig. 21-16. "Evolution," a custom showpiece featuring padded vinyl trim around portholes, op-art design motif, and fade out murals (paint and murals by Carl Caiati).

242

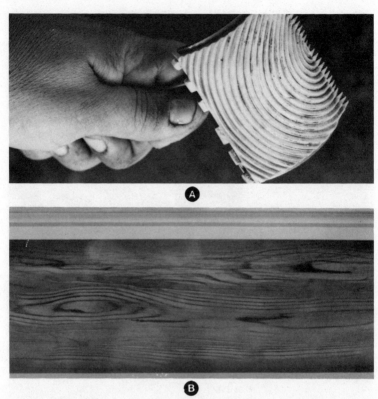

Fig. 21-17. Wood graining tool (A) and wood grain effect (B).

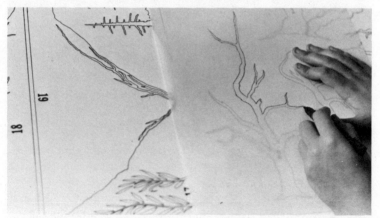

Fig. 21-18. A traceable stencil-making kit simplifies stencil production. It is available from Badger Airbrush Company and can be purchased at better art supply stores.

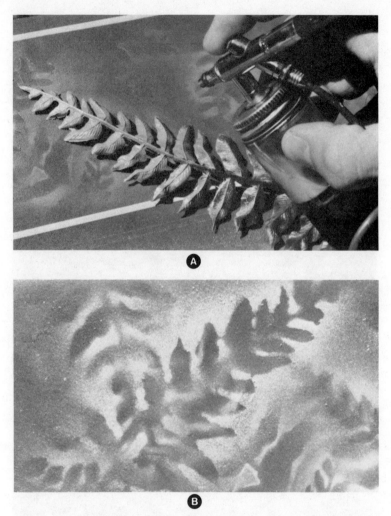

Fig. 21-19. Simple design motifs can be made using an imitation plastic fern (A). Overlapping the ferns and airbrushing through them creates an effect as in (B).

plied wet over the light brown coat. Then the wood grain squeegee is pulled or wiped across the still wet, diluted acrylic enamel with a rocking motion to create the grain and knot effects.

If the effect is not intense enough or if you goof on the first attempt, the enamel reducer and entire graining procedure is executed anew. Wood graining is so simple and foolproof that positive results can almost be guaranteed. Wood graining is an excellent

Fig. 21-20. Close-up detailing of some of the mural renderings of Shelby Goode.

basic starting exercise for the novice or beginning painter.

Custom painting, just like any project presented in this book, is well within the realm of the do-it-yourself van buff. Breaking it all down into simple steps makes the job easy to tackle (Figs. 21-18, 21-19A, and 21-19B). If you can follow instructions to the letter and practice until you attain expertise, painting your van can be a fulfilling project (Fig. 21-20).

Chapter 22

Vans for Show and Go

Custom vans have developed into two basic categories: show and go. The show van or show custom usually features full outer murals or custom paint jobs. These are made possible by the use of small windows, ports, or no windows at all so as not to infringe on mural or design space. If you're not partial to murals, you may cover the outer expanses with tasteful, well-thought-out graphics that can also be aesthetically pleasing. Show van interiors are usually more lavish than they are functional, stressing mood decor, mood lighting, sophisticated fabrics, and interior decorator type motifs.

The go van is the more functional counterpart even though it may also abound in show features. The go van will most likely have large bay windows, interior travel and sleeping facilities for comfort, sink, cooking, and refrigeration facilities, etc. Outer modifications may include a raised top, luggage rack on roof, and basic graphic paint work to minimize the commercial truck look (Fig. 22-1).

The contemporary van has metamorphosed from the mindblowing "motel-on-wheels" to a more sedate (but highly original), everyday family vehicle. It can be a second, long-range travel and recreational vehicle that can also be used for everyday transportation, shopping, etc. With the cubic interior capacity offered, you can go on a shopping spree and go in style. On weekends, the family can "head for the hills" with their own comfortable sleeping

Fig. 22-1. A basic recreational cruiser with simple but effective paint treatment.

quarters, an impossibility with even the largest standard automobiles (Fig. 22-2).

The magnificent vans presented and displayed in this chapter cover many aspects of custom van design. They run the gamut from basic but sophisticated simplicity to mind boggling, budget-breaking lavishness.

Fig. 22-2. "Hump's Longhorn," a go machine with mild show flavoring.

Fig. 22-3. A simple, tasteful go van paint motif (courtesy Glastop, Inc.).

GLASTOP INC. VANS

The go vans, everyday and recreational customs, are presented with many stylish adaptations and variances (Fig. 22-3). Of particular note are the magnificent interiors designed and constructed by Glastop Inc., Pompano Beach, Florida.

Glastop is renowned throughout custom recreational circles as the finest builders of functional and artistic van creations. Quality materials and designs combined with flawless workmanship have led many to consider them the best in the business. Their credits include simple interiors for the average middle-class American, a retinue of vans for the Saudi Arabian Air Force, and quality showpieces that have garnished honors in custom shows and on the streets (Fig. 22-4).

Bob White and Dave Beal are the excellent cabinetmakers as well as the principals and owners at Glastop. They do a major part of their fabrication in fine woods and Formica with exquisite detailing throughout. A major part of their custom work involves installing pop tops and sport cruiser roof extensions. They are the local distributors of quality Viking fiberglass extension tops. The magnitude of their custom craftsmanship is best illustrated by the representative photos in this chapter (Fig. 22-5).

GARRISON CUSTOM VANS

One cannot talk about show customs without bringing up the name of Garrison Custom of Waterbury-Thomaston, Connecticut. Gary Garrison is one of the most astute and prolific customizers in the country, recognized for his innovative genius and superior craftsmanship (Fig. 22-6). Not satisfied with simple or bolt-on

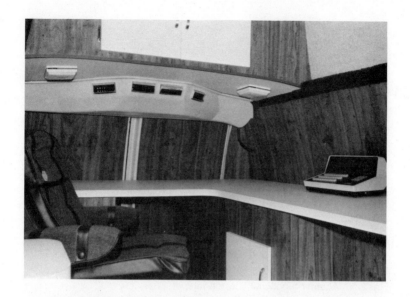

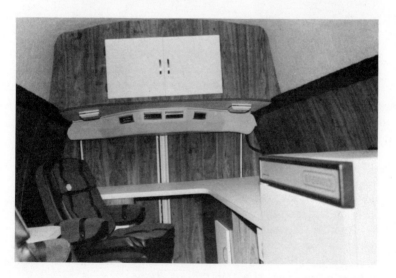

Fig. 22-4. Executive van interior (courtesy Glastop, Inc.).

modification techniques, Garrison fabricates and designs his own parts to coordinate with his wildly styled, all-out showpieces. A welder and steel fabricator by trade, Garrison also is a prominent artist, and his murals and paint work have graced a multitude of custom cars, vans, and motorcycles that have taken top show honors

Fig. 22-5. Another functional Glastop interior.

in paint, design, and craftsmanship. A number of his endeavors grace and glorify these pages. One unfinished one is his own personal show vehicle. Another is the outcome of a collaborative effect undertaken with Carl Caiati.

Gary did all the custom steel fabrication on Caiati's "Apocalypse" van (Figs. 22-7 and 22-8). Mingling some of his design expertise with Caiati's, the outcome is a show-winning custom that started out as a 64 GMC. "Apocalypse" features an extended front nose piece (á la Garrison) that houses a Mercury Cougar front grille and headlight piece, making this one of the few custom vans with flip-up headlights (Fig. 22-9). The back doors were discarded and the back was finished off as a solid unit using welded-on steel sheeting that houses a Thunderbird taillight (Fig. 22-10).

Another Garrison custom van, still in its embryonic stages, is shown in Fig. 22-11. Though not complete, you can see the innovative, quality craftsmanship typical of Gary. Some of his paint work is also exhibited within these pages.

"CLOSE ENCOUNTERS" VAN

When discussing paint work, one cannot overlook Shelby Goode of Naranja, Florida. Shelby is a fine artist and sublime muralist as evidenced by his mural magic on the "Close Encounters" van (Fig. 22-12). Close-ups of Shelby's detailing can also be seen in the custom paint section (Fig. 22-13).

Fig. 22-6. "Space Odyssey," a fantasy paint creation by Gary Garrison.

BADGER "STAR BUS"

Bob Leyrer one of the finest of interior designers, is also well represented, as he should be. His workmanship and design for the Badger "Star Bus" is unsurpassed; he is an excellent interior decorator (Fig. 22-14).

The last and featured attraction in this chapter is the Badger

Fig. 22-7. "Apocalypse" van with trick paint.

"Star Bus," built for and owned by the Badger Airbrush Co., Franklin Park, Illinois (Fig. 22-15).

The "Star Bus" was designed on a "money-is-no-object" basis. This $30,000 showpiece was conceived to promote and illustrate

Fig. 22-8. "Apocalypse" an interior with crushed velvet couch, wood paneling, and chrome plastic divider.

252

Fig. 22-9. The rear of "Apocalypse" sports a Thunderbird taillight lens in a custom steel frame (by Garrison).

Fig. 22-10. Front view of "Apocalypse." Garrison fashioned an extended nose piece and housed a Ford Cougar front grille and headlights in it.

Fig. 22-11. Another Garrison custom in early stages. A totally unique, individualized concept.

the virtues of Badger Airbrushes, hence the dynamic exterior paint styling and muralization. The paint and mural work was the joint effort of Sliique and Carl Caiati. Sliique, a custom painter of nationwide fame, is responsible for many show trophies attributable to her airbrush expertise.

In addition to paint, the van, a 1978 short wheelbase Ford Econoline, underwent some extensive exterior customizing. Spoiler, flares, sunvisor, and running boards, all fiberglass from Imaginary Glass, were added. To intensify the outer space theme, a Van Trekk

Fig. 22-12. The "Close Encounters" Ford show van (paint by Shelby Goode).

Fig. 22-13. "Jungle Fantasy" van (paint by Shelby Goode).

grille and Trekk rear window shades by PVT Plastics were installed. Turbine-type ET Wheels were used to accommodate the wide Pro-Track 60 tires. The van roof was covered in black padded vinyl. Side ports and sunroof are from Stretch Forming Corp. (Fig. 22-16).

The opulent interior, brainchild of Leyrer, is as formidable as the exterior. The interior decor is primarily natural Brazilian rosewood, retailing at $98 per sheet, integrated with button-tufted,

Fig. 22-14. Classic contoured crushed velvet couch in the Badger "Star Bus."

Fig. 22-15. The Badger "Star Bus," built for the Badger Airbrush Company. Design by Bob Leyrer, paint by Carl Caiati and Sliique.

light blue crushed velvet.

The rosewood entertainment console and bar unit against the rear passenger side wall also houses an Akai reel-to-reel tape deck amplified with a Sherwood 70-watt amp. The music producing components feed a speaker system housed in the rear corner ceiling of the van. This is one of two sound systems in the van and works on 110 volt ac (of great value at custom shows). The second sound system is comprised of an AM-FM Mitsubishi cassette stereo unit,

Fig. 22-16. The Badger "Star Bus." This view displays a mirror sunk into the ceiling (designer, Bob Leyrer).

256

overhead console mounted and wired into a quad speaker setup. The speakers are two rear, corner-mounted, 6×9 Mitsubishi SG-69CB coaxial speakers and two Mitsubishi SR-35WA round, dual cone, downward facing units mounted in the overhead console at the front of the driver's compartment.

Also housed in the overhead console is a Kris XL-50 CB transceiver and digital clock. Instrumentation is all Stewart-Warner. Seating is graced with blue velvet fabric matching the decor velvet in texture and color, custom built by Frank of Florida Van Seats, Ft. Lauderdale, Florida.

In its entirety, the Badger "Star Bus" is rhapsody of custom grandeur—a compilation of many refined techniques coordinated into a fine representative custom package.

Chapter 23

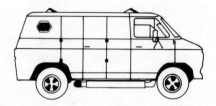

Minivans

Hot on the heels of the van craze comes the minivan. This newest hot wheel setup is the forerunner in the van movement of the 1980s. Though not as spacious as the standard van, the mini offers a feasible alternative. It has many of the formidable concepts of larger vans, but is scaled down to make it an ideal everyday vehicle. New structural concepts as well as progressive styling make the minivan an acceptable vehicle whose popularity is growing from day to day.

The compact van idea is not totally new. The Europeans have greatly favored the scaled-down versions, such as the original Volkswagen minibus that gained much popularity in the 60s and 70s, though it was overshadowed by the standard Ford, Chevy, and Dodge cargo vans that dominated the van scene in those eras.

A great pro factor of the minivan is its lower gas consumption, a factor to consider in your budget. Second is the inner capacity that makes the station wagon, once also popular, a thing of the past. The mini is more spaciously designed, offering better headroom as well as storage space.

Realizing the impact of the new vehicle format, all the major automobile manufacturers decided to fortify the craze, offering some new, highly stylized, street-worthy machines. Figure 23-1 shows a typical popular van of the day and its relative size and space comparisons to the station wagon and the standard cargo wagon.

In this chapter, we will present the major minivan offerings.

1984 DODGE CARAVAN

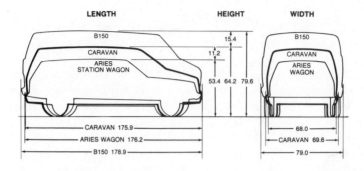

DIMENSIONS IN INCHES

Fig. 23-1. The Dodge Caravan fits neatly between the station wagon and the standard cargo wagon (courtesy Dodge).

We will show their relative differences and specific advantages that may vary from model to model.

VOLKSWAGEN VANAGON

Volkswagen has come a long way from its original minibus concept and is currently capitalizing on its Vanagon. Changes to the 1985 seven-seat Vanagon (Fig. 23-2), which has one of the largest carrying capacities of any minivan sold in the United States, include a new padded dashboard with built-in shelf, map/glove com-

Fig. 23-2. The 1985 Volkswagen Vanagon GL (courtesy Volkswagen of America, Inc.).

259

partment light, and standard tinted glass. Also, operation of the sliding door (a feature pioneered by VW in 1967) has been made quieter and easier.

Both the Vanagon and Vanagon GL are full seven-seat "garageable" vans with a great deal of luggage space. They can be ordered with factory-installed air conditioning, Heidelberg AM/FM auto-reverse cassette stereo with four speakers, automatic transmission, metallic paint, and rear window wiper/washer. A new optional "Weekender Package" includes a folding rear bench seat that converts into a double bed with storage compartment, engine compartment cushion, and a center seat with a folding backrest.

Inspired by the success of specially equipped Wolfsburg Edition Vanagons offered in mid 1984, VW has made power-assisted steering with a smaller diameter padded wheel standard on the top-of-the-line Vanagon GL. The 1985 GL model also has the padded dashboard with map/glove compartment light, an illuminated passenger sunvisor mirror, longer front seat bottom cushions, aerodynamic wheel covers, and a wide beltline stripe to compliment the large selection of new exterior colors.

The only factory-built, fully self-contained camper on the market, the Vanagon Camper (Fig. 23-3), gets a "GL" designation

Fig. 23-3. The 1985 Volkswagen Vanagon GL Camper (courtesy Volkswagen of America, Inc.).

Fig. 23-4. The interior view of the Vanagon GL Camper (courtesy Volkswagen of America, Inc.).

for 1985. With it comes many of the GL's luxury and convenience features, such as power steering, aerostyle wheel covers, tachometer with LCD clock, longer front seat cushions, and lighted passenger sunvisor mirror.

The Vanagon GL Camper also has velour upholstery, front seats that swivel with fold-down armrests, and a redesigned storage cabinet behind the driver's seat that permits a greater seat recline angle. Factory-installed air conditioning, automatic transmission, metallic paint, rear window wiper/washer, and a new removable center swivel seat with fold-down armrests that increases the Camper's seating capacity from four to five are available as options (Fig. 23-4).

All Vanagons are powered by a quiet, efficient, water-cooled engine mounted over the rear drive wheels for maximum traction. Fuel injection, four-wheel independent suspension, rack-and-pinion steering, and power-assisted front disc brakes are also part of the Vanagon's standard specifications.

The GL Camper features a "pop-up" top, two full-sized beds, screens and curtains for windows, running water, a propane stove, and a refrigerator that operates on 12 volts, 110 volts, or propane. Hanging lockers and cupboards provide plenty of storage for food, clothing, and vacation necessities. There is also a luggage rack located over the driving compartment for bulky items. It can be reached through the screen window in the pop-up top.

RENAULT

Much to everyone's surprise, Renault came on with a worthy contender, the Espace minivan, which has gained much popularity in Europe. At present, the front-wheel drive Espace featuring a 110-hp, 4-cylinder engine is capable of achieving more than 40 miles per gallon of gas. In 1986, AMC will begin importing the Renault mini, which is similar in profile to the Ford Aerostar. The Espace will comfortably carry seven passengers and take up little garage space with its overall height of 65 inches and width of 70 inches. Wide doors of the 167-inch long, 2,650-pound vehicle open easily and close tightly with front seating offering full swivel capabilities. Select Renault dealers will be the 1986 and future source of the very fashionable "Espace."

CHRYSLER

Spurred on by its phenomenal growth under Lee Iacocca, Chrysler saturated the market and received wide acclaim for the Dodge Caravan and Plymouth Voyager minivans. The mini's feature superb styling and many formidable innovations (see Figs. 23-5 through 23-14).

Fig. 23-5. The Dodge Caravan is a front-wheel drive, multipurpose vehicle (courtesy Dodge).

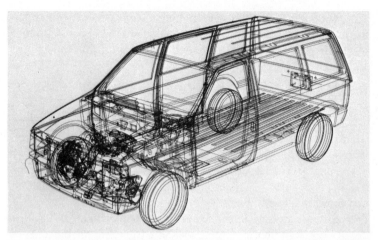

Fig. 23-6. The computer drawing of the 1984 Dodge Caravan shows the position of the transversely-mounted front-wheel drive engine and transaxle (courtesy Dodge).

In addition to roomy minivan size, the Chrysler offerings feature a very desirable front-wheel drive, allowing a flat front floor with a carlike step-up of 14 inches. With the drivetrain entirely in the front, engine noise is reduced and the entire package emulates a car rather than a truck. In lieu of attaining EPA fuel economy figures, the base Chrysler vans have been outfitted with a 2.56 overall final drive gear ratio. Fifth gear may be a bit sluggish on

Fig. 23-7. Plymouth Voyager (courtesy Chrysler/Plymouth).

hills, but overall, the 2.2-liter engine package offers excellent performance. The automatic should be considered over the manual until Chrysler regears the manual transmission as planned in 1985-86.

DODGE CARAVAN

Standard engine on the Caravan is a 2.2-liter 4-cylinder engine, with a larger 2.6-liter four-cylinder engine available. A five-speed manual or three-speed automatic transmission are available.

All models equipped with five-speed manual transaxles feature a new "fuel pacer" Shift Indicator Light. This device signals the driver when to shift gears for optimum fuel economy and can increase fuel economy a projected 1 mile per gallon.

An optional floor-mounted, lockable front storage bin and console provides increase storage capacity in 1985 model Caravans. Premium models may be equipped with an overhead storage console mounted on the ceiling between the front bucket seats.

Measuring 175.9 inches overall and just 64.2 inches high, the Caravan provides an amazing degree of roominess, comfort, and versatility, Fig. 23-15. It glides easily in and out of parking spaces, through car washes, and fits conveniently in standard garages. The 1985 Caravan weighs slightly less than 3,000 pounds.

In addition to the Convert-a-bed and forward locking consoles, options on the 1985 Caravan include new 14-inch aluminum road

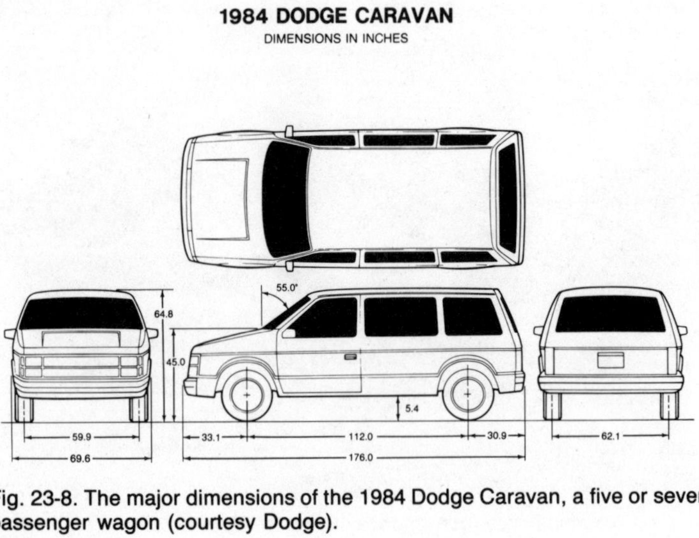

1984 DODGE CARAVAN
DIMENSIONS IN INCHES

64.8   45.0   55.0°   5.4

59.9   69.6   33.1   112.0   30.9   176.0   62.1

Fig. 23-8. The major dimensions of the 1984 Dodge Caravan, a five or seven-passenger wagon (courtesy Dodge).

264

1984 CARAVAN SEATING CONFIGURATIONS

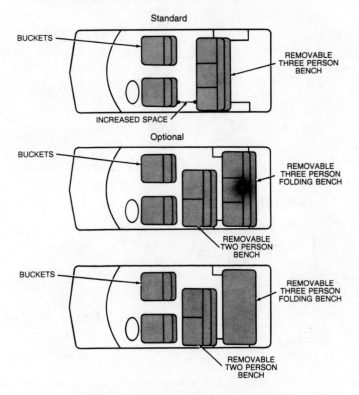

Fig. 23-9. The versatile Dodge Caravan offers a variety of seating arrangements (courtesy Dodge).

wheels, vinyl bodyside molding, front and rear bumper guards, electrically-powered remote control sideview mirrors, and Ultimate Sound AM Stereo and FM Stereo electronically-tuned radio.

PLYMOUTH VOYAGER

The Voyager provides seating for up to seven, low step-in height, riding comfort, nimble handling, excellent visibility, and fuel economy, Fig. 23-16. It has walk-through capability and is "garageable." Although 39 inches shorter than a full-size wagon, it offers 40 percent more luggage space. New options for '85 are a front overhead console, a lockable forward console, and a Convert-a-bed bench seat. A three-place front bench also is available.

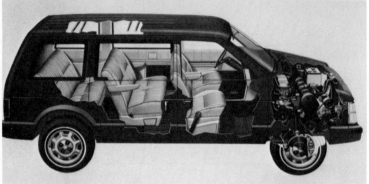

Fig. 23-10. The Plymouth Voyager is ideal for family transportation, recreation, or business use (courtesy Chrysler/Plymouth).

The base Voyager, with front bucket seats and a three-place bench seat, has a 2.2-liter engine. five-speed manual transmission, power steering, and electrically-tuned AM radio with integral digital clock as standard equipment. A three-speed automatic with the 2.2-liter engine is optional in five-passenger vehicles.

The medium priced Voyager SE offers an upgraded interior, increased seating capacity, and a two-tone paint package. The premium Voyager LE has luxurious high-back bucket seats, two-tone paint or woodgrain exterior, and a more extensive list of standard equipment. A 2.6-liter automatic drivetrain is optional.

New features in 1985 include:

- Power dual outside mirrors option.
- "Ultimate Sound" radio system with new AM stereo and FM stereo available.

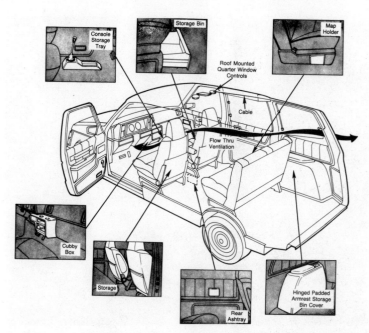

Fig. 23-11. Extra touches in the Dodge Caravan include built-in storage space and roof-mounted controls to adjust rear quarter windows without leaving your seat (courtesy Dodge).

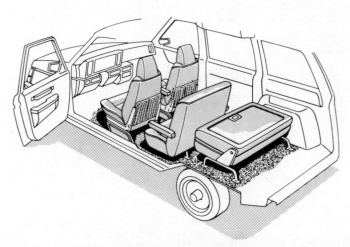

Fig. 23-12. Dodge Caravan's fold-down rear seat provides a firm surface for storage and can be moved fore and aft 6 1/2 inches for increased luggage space. The second and third seats can also be removed (courtesy Dodge).

Fig. 23-13. Instrument panel of the 1984 Dodge Caravan (courtesy Dodge).

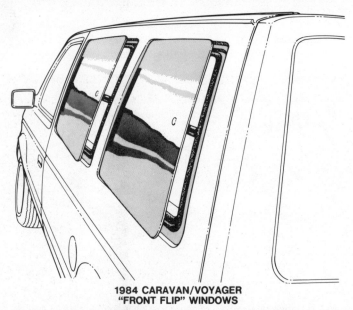

**1984 CARAVAN/VOYAGER
"FRONT FLIP" WINDOWS**

Fig. 23-14. The side windows of the Dodge Caravan are tinted glass and hinged at the front with a "flip out" latch at the rear (courtesy Dodge).

Fig. 23-15. The Dodge Caravan (courtesy Dodge).

- Convert-a-bed capability option.
- Overhead console (LE) option.
- Lockable forward console option.
- Bench front seat option (Voyager and SE).
- Three new exterior colors and one new interior color.
- Fourteen-inch plastic wheel cover option (SE, LE).
- Redesign of aluminum wheel in Sport Wheel Package.
- New Popular Equipment (SE, LE), Luxury Equipment (LE), and Travel Equipment (SE, LE) Discount Package options available.

Fig. 23-16. The Plymouth Voyager (courtesy Chrysler/Plymouth).

The "Magic Camper Package" has a new family-sized tent that attaches directly to the side door opening of the vehicle. It also includes a Convert-a-bed bench seat, a lockable forward storage console, roof luggage rack, sunscreen window glass, a 20-gallon fuel tank, a 500-amp battery, heavy-duty suspension, styled road wheels, and steel-belted all-weather radial tires.

In a special introductory offer, the $500 value tent will be given free to customers ordering the Magic Camper Package option, which soon will be on display at major auto and camper shows and available for spring delivery. The key feature in the package is the large, lightweight tent that provides a fully-enclosed camping unit with a T-shaped floor plan when attached to the sliding side door opening of the Voyager. The tent is attached to the Voyager by an enclosed passageway, providing walk-through access into the vehicle. It also can be detached and used as a free-standing unit when the Voyager is needed for running errands. The spacious Magic Tent is constructed from nylon taffeta with a one-piece, "rip stop" polyethylene floor. It's unique curvilinear design provides a spacious 6-feet 4 inches of center headroom and 5-feet high walls. It measures 8 feet × 10 feet overall and can sleep four comfortably, plus two in the Voyager's Convert-a-bed.

The tent has a double roof which provides air pocket insulation to repel the sun's heat. The outer layer is urethane treated to keep out moisture. The inner panel is made from breathable taffeta to enhance ventilation.

Spacious front and rear doors measure 5 feet, 3 inches high by 5 feet wide and feature zippered nylon mesh screen doors and full storm flaps. The zippers are self-mending nylon coil design.

The large windows provide nearly 5 square feet of ventilating space on each of the tent and have inner closing flaps. A fly leaf overhang protects the windows from roof moisture runoff.

The Magic Tent is connected to the Voyager by a fully enclosed urethane coated passageway. It is fully sealed to the sliding door opening by Velcro stripping. A large 5-foot, 5-inch canopy shields the passageway roof to guard against moisture pooling. It is secured to the Voyager's roof drip rails by urethane-coated hooks. A matching roll-up canopy can be extended above the front doorway to provide weather protection or shade.

Framing for the tent is provided by 7/8-inch diameter lightweight aluminum tubing. The corner tethering loops, which secure it to the ground, can withstand a 100-pound pull.

To enhance ventilation of the entire tent and vehicle, the tent comes with three nylon mesh screens that fit over the Voyager's front windows and the left rear pop-out window. The screens feature magnetic stripping, which lock them tight to the Voyager's exterior panels.

A matching urethane-coated zippered pouch is provided to protect the opened sliding door from weather when the Magic Tent is attached. The Magic Tent also features nylon web markers that extend from the tent to show the driver exactly where to spot his Voyager relative to the tent's rear door opening.

The tent package fits into a pouch that is only 11 inches in diameter. It weighs less than 25 pounds and can fit easily on the floor between the Voyager's wheel wells. The free tent offer extends through the 1985 model year.

The Magic Camper Package is available only for the Voyager SE model. All items in the camper package can be ordered individually as options except the tent.

CHEVROLET AND GMC

GM has stuck to the basic van design concept that make the GM Safari and Chevy Astro van smaller counterparts of the basic standard GM cargo vans. A large mini, the Astro and Safari have about 25 more cubic feet of room than the Chrysler mini and 1.3 cubic feet more than the Toyota van; most of this space made possible through the GM and Chevy vans height.

Featured on the GM vans are front engine placement with rear

Fig. 23-17. The new-size Chevrolet Astro has rear-wheel drive (courtesy Chevrolet).

271

Fig. 23-18. The Chevy Astro Van (courtesy Chevrolet).

wheel drive (Fig. 23-17). The Chevy Astro and GM Safari (Figs. 23-18, 23-19) use a front subframe to house the engine, which is in turn bolted to a unitized body. Two engine options are offered, an economical four-cylinder and a less economical but more powerful V-6.

GM Minis are available in two models. The passenger version

Fig. 23-19. A see-through view of the Astro (courtesy Chevrolet).

seats up to eight adults in comfort and luxury (more than any other small van). A cargo version provides the muscle to carry up to 1,700 pounds of payload (also tops).

Safari and Astro feature a greater towing capacity, larger cargo capacity, and more engine power than the minivans now on the market. It's the product of a $600 million investment and incorporates many innovative design and development concepts (Fig. 23-20).

They contain the rear-wheel drive a working truck, towing vehicle, or loaded passenger van needs for good traction and gradeability. They also have 151.1 cubic feet of cargo space; a sliding side door for tight-quarters convenience; swing-open rear doors for easy loading; and the optional high-tech Vortec V6 engine (Fig. 23-21).

Under the hood is a choice of standard "Tech IV" or optional "Vortec V6" power—the 4.3-liter V6 being an all-new engine that delivers more horsepower and more torque. The 2.5-liter Tech IV's computer-controlled electronic fuel-injection system helps save money by precisely metering the right amount of fuel into the engine. With a manual four-speed transmission, Tech IV delivers an EPA-estimated 22 miles per gallon city/26 miles per gallon

Fig. 23-20. The Chevy Astro Van is available in three trailering classifications: light, for up to 2,000 pounds; medium, up to 4,000 pounds; and heavy, up to 5,000 pounds (courtesy Chevrolet).

Fig. 23-21. The slab-side Astro Van is perfect for commercial use (courtesy Chevrolet).

highway. This economical—yet strong—combination, coupled with the large optional 27-gallon fuel tank, means a highway cruising rate of 702 miles is possible.

For power, the optional Vortec V6 is the strongest engine in its class, generating 145 hp. and 225 lbs./ft. of torque. Fuel economy is an impressive 18 mpg city/24 mpg highway for the automatic four-speed with overdrive.

The power of the Vortec V6 means a net payload of 1,700 pounds for the commercial version. When properly equipped, an Astro with the 4.3-liter Vortec V6 has a towing capacity, including trailer, cargo, and passengers, of up to 5,000 pounds.

Astro's high fuel efficiency is due in part to lengthy aerodynamic testing in the GM Aerodynamics Laboratory where its design was shaped to get through the wind on a minimum amount of horsepower. The front end was specially contoured to cut wind resistance. With a drag coefficient of 0.38-making it the sleekest vehicle of its kind-Astro has a lower drag coefficient than many sports cars.

Four seating configurations are available in the Astro passenger van—from four when the Astro is equipped with bucket seats in front (Fig. 23-22) and midship, to eight with front bucket seats and two bench seats. Multiple seating ability is just the beginning of the story when it comes to making passengers comfortable. With the flick of a few latches, Astro's bench seating configurations can be arranged. The middle and optional rear bench seats can be completely removed or reconfigured to face each other or face forward or rearward.

About 6 feet from road to roof (73.7 inches passenger, 74.5 inches cargo), the Astro has 4 feet (48 inches) of walk-through space inside. It is 77 inches wide on the outside—3 inches less than Chevy's conventional vans—but seating dimensions are almost identical.

Astro and Safari Specifications

Power train type	rear-wheel drive
Base engine	2.5-liter L4 with EFI
Optional engine	4.3-liter 4-bbl. V6
Base transmission	4-speed manual
Optional transmissions	4-speed automatic with overdrive
EPA-estimated fuel economy with standard engine and transmission	
Cargo Van:	22 city/26 highway mpg*
Passenger Van:	22 city/26 highway mpg*
Fuel tank capacity	
Standard	17 gallons
Optional	27 gallons
Seating	
Cargo Van base seating	one

Fig. 23-22. This top-of-the-line Chevy Astro CL is designed for maximum efficiency that puts the driver in charge (courtesy Chevrolet).

Cargo Van available seating	two or four
Passenger base seating	five
Passenger available seating	four, seven, or eight
Available towing capacity	2,000 or 5,000 lbs.
Rear door type	two panel doors
Wheelbase	111.0 inches
Overall length	176.8 inches
Width	77.0 inches
Height	
Passenger	73.7 inches
Cargo	74.5 inches

FORD AEROSTAR

Ford, continuously coming out with new ideas, has another winner in the Aerostar minivan. Ford designs the Aerostar to appeal almost equally to customers seeking personal transportation and those interested in carrying cargo (Figs. 23-23 to 23-25).

The Aerostar's standard powerplant, an electronically fuel-injected 2.3-liter engine with computer controls, combines peppy performance with fuel economy projected at 26 mpg city and 30 mpg highway. It is positioned between full-size vans like the Ford Econoline and passenger car station wagons like the Ford LTD and Country Squire. Ford's minivan has room for seven people or a max-

Fig. 23-23. The sleekest lines of any vehicle in its class belongs to the Ford Aerostar (courtesy Ford).

Fig. 23-24. The Ford Aerostar's sleek good looks, roominess, garageability, and fuel economy appeals to young families (courtesy Ford).

Fig. 23-25. The Ford Aerostar will appeal to van users who want a down-sized vehicle with maneuverability, top payload, and towing power, coupled with fuel economy (courtesy Ford).

imum cargo space of 175.9 cubic feet, with payloads up to 2,000 pounds. With optional 2.8-liter V6 power, the Aerostar can tow trailers up to 5,000 pounds. Standard transmission is a five-speed manual overdrive, with four-speed automatic overdrive optional.

Innovative features include aluminum driveline components to reduce upsprung weight and to contribute to ride quality. Aerostar's 119-inch wheelbase, longest in its class, and computer-designed suspension promote a smooth highway ride and enhance towing capability. Efficient use of interior space gives Aerostar more leg room at all seating positions than in front-wheel-drive competitive vans with slightly greater overall length.

Aerostar has a computer-designed, low-profile instrument panel with electronic instrument cluster and multicolor liquid crystal displays included on wagons with XL and XLT trim. Optional air conditioning is available with an auxiliary rear-action cooling system. Optional six-speaker "OmniSound" stereo includes rear-compartment controls and headphone jacks.

TOYOTA MINIVAN

The most radical of the minis, the mid-engined Toyota mini, sports the most distinctive and probably the most aesthetic styling. For looks and lines it is hard to beat (Fig. 23-26).

In 1985, Toyota made available to the minivan set three ad-

Fig. 23-26. The Toyota Van LE's plush interior and new wheels add to its sporty look (Toyota Motor Sales).

mirable models: the LE van, Deluxe van, and Cargo van. All of the models include the peppy 2.0-liter OHV four-cylinder Toyota engine with electronic fuel injection. The 1998-cc powerplant comes from the 2-liter mill that Toyota has successfully utilized in Japanese taxi cabs, with the addition of fuel injection for improved driveability. The fuel injection allows smoother and more positive throttle response with no flat spots in the power band.

The powerplant itself produces 90 hp. at 4400 rpm. and 120 ft/lbs of torque at 3000 rpm. The engine, amidships, is accessible through a panel beneath the driver's seat. Changes of oil are required at only 10,000-mile intervals, and the platinum-tipped spark plugs will allegedly last 60,000 miles. In essence, from 1985 on, the LE model delivers better mileage than the 1984 forerunner Toyota minis.

Due to the weight distribution and mid-engine mounting, the mini-marvel handles superbly. The brakes are not exceedingly grabby, but the van does exhibit front-end dip coupled with rear-end lift under extremely fast and hard-braking conditions. Though the operator's seat is situated high over the engine compartment, driver comfort is in no way sacrificed. Seats are well contoured offering firm support with comfort adjustments; the models from 1985 on feature a fold-down armrest. In the driving compartment, all of the controls are readily accessible, and the large windshield offers an unlimited field of view. A welcome addition are the finest rearview mirrors ever to be offered on a vehicle, electrically operated and vibration free.

The Toyota minivan displays the unquestionable Toyota quality prevalent in all their automotive lines. Door fit and finish is excellent with infinite attention given to quality control in construction inside and out. The Toyota, especially the exclusive LE model, is not cheap, but neither is the quality of the vehicle. For styling and quality it has to be the best minivan offering on the market.

Specifications (LE Model)

Curb Weight	2955 lb.
Cargo Volume	149.8 cu. ft.
Wheelbase	88 in.
Track, front/rear	56.1/54.3 in.
Powertrain	1998cc OHC, four
	Electronic Fuel Injection
	5-spd. manual

BHP/RPM	90 @ 4400
Torque/RPM	120 @ 3000
Axle Ratio	3.909:1

Performance

0-30 mph	4.94
0-60 mph	16.22
1/4 mile, sec	19.80
1/4 mile, speed, mph	67.4
45-60 passing	N/A
Indicated 60 mph is actually	61
Braking, 55-0	134 ft.
MPG, V & T Observed	23

Front suspension is comprised of a double wishbone configuration, including gas-filled shock absorbers, upper torsion bars, and front stabilizing bar. An independent suspension system in the rear also features gas-filled shocks coiled springs and stabilizing bar. Even at the higher road speeds, the unique suspension system smoothes out the ride admirably, minimizing road surface irregularities.

As an option, a manually-operated front moonroof is offered. Other options include automatic transmission, power and tilt steering wheel, cruise control, dual air conditioning, sunroof, ice maker, aluminum wheels, and two-tone paint.

Chapter 24

Customizing Minivans

With their sleek, road sharp styling, the new minivans lend themselves readily to custom additive components and decor. As is the case with standard vans, many van converters concentrate on providing customizing facilities and specialized interior-exterior fabrication.

Readers seriously considering minivan conversion or services offered by national minivan converters may want to obtain a copy of the *1985 Buyer's Guide to Van Conversion*. The guide explains what is available, by whom, and how to contact various manufacturers directly. The price for the Guide is $3.00 and it may be obtained from:

Hanley Publishing Co.
3412 Main St.
Skokie, IL 60076

DIRECT CONNECTION

Those of you who are familiar with Chrysler will know of their Direct Connection facilities. This segment of the corporation is dedicated to offering custom parts and accessories for Dodge vehicles and engines. The success of the Dodge Supervan T-115 prompted Chrysler to stock parts and additive accessories that can significantly upgrade and enhance the appearance of the Chrysler minis.

One great accessory offering is the mini-Ram dam, a front spoiler unit tailor-made to fit into the design lines of the T-115 front end. The air dam features driving/fog light mounting holes and cooling ducts to impart a "racy" look. To complement the air dam, side skirts and a rear pan section are being designed in addition to a roof mount rear wing spoiler similar to the wings once offered by G.M. for Firebirds and Camaros. The body pieces are injection-molded plastic, presumably polyurethane like the body panel components available for front-wheel drive Chrysler compacts.

Direct Connection also offers minivan interior, preformed, add-on panels. They provide a clean, functional, finished interior far more attractive than the bare metal unfinished look.

For more information on Direct Connection minivan parts, contact:

Direct Connection Center
20026 Progress Drive
Strongsville, OH 44136

Four-wheel drive for a minivan? Not in factory issue, but there are services that will successfully and exactingly convert minis to four-wheel drive.

One very successful and reputable company is Overland Manufacturing located in Newburyport, Massachusetts. Overland has gained a far-reaching reputation for converting full-sized vans to four-wheel drive since 1977. Overland also includes a 12-month, 12,000-mile warranty on parts and labor not covered by manufacturers.

The Overland Dodge mini four-wheel drive conversion is very popular. The operation is complex but feasible. Existing engine, transaxle, and front-end components are removed from the stock van. A 2.6-liter Mitsubishi engine (either manual or auto transaxle) and transfer case from a Dodge Power Ram 50-minitruck replaces stock issue. A special jig designed by Overland positions the D-50 4 × 4 independent front suspension, axles, and steering box and linkage during the installation. When in proper alignment the subframe is mig-welded onto the minivan's unibody frame. Transfer case and front torsion bars are then installed, and heavy-duty leaf springs are mounted to the heavy-duty, six-lug rear axle. In construction, ride height of body and suspension can be adjusted according to the customer's requirements.

In addition to Chrysler, Overland provides four-wheel conver-

CONCEPT I EXTERIOR

CONCEPT I INTERIOR

Fig. 24-1. Cars & Concepts offers a Concept I special vehicle conversion for Dodge Caravan and Plymouth Voyager vans (courtesy Cars & Concepts).

sion for Chevy Astro and Ford Aerostar Minis. Full particulars may be obtained by writing to:

Overland Manufacturing
345 Merrimac Street
Newburyport, MA 01950

Cars & Concepts has long been an automotive accessory and conversion dealer specializing in custom sunroof installations, T-top manufacturing, and accessory parts sales. Their reputation and quality is unbeatable.

In the minivan custom field, they offer their Concept I special vehicle conversion for Dodge Caravan and Plymouth Voyager vans

(Fig. 24-1). Dressing up the exterior are the front air dam and side panel accessory additives that can be seen in Fig. 24-2. To embellish the exterior package, Concept I features accent body stripes and auxiliary driving lamps.

The interior package include premium carpeting and upholstery (button-tufted velour covering on custom captain's seats), a removable center seat, refrigerator/heater, enclosed sidewall storage compartments, custom lighting, folding table, Deluxe wood trim, driver console, and privacy blinds.

The Concept I conversion is produced with quality of materials and construction. Cars & Concepts provides the customer with a 12-month, 12,000-mile limited warranty on materials and workmanship. For more information contact:

Cars & Concepts
12500 E. Grand Avenue
Brighton, MI 48116

Check also with your local Chrysler dealers who may offer the Concept I package.

WHEELS FOR MINIVANS

The prime custom additive for minivans (as with all vehicles) is the custom or mag wheels. Custom mags that grace the minis

Fig. 24-2. To embellish the exterior package, Concept I features accent body stripes and auxiliary driving lamps (courtesy Cars & Concepts).

Fig. 24-3. The Cragar "Quick Trick" is a chrome and matte mag featuring the popular perforated wheel (courtesy Cragar).

and improve their appearance are easily obtained from H.D. Rose and similar automotive specialty outlets. The following units are some of the newer offerings that have generated acclaim among the minivan set.

Fig. 24-4. The Solar-10 by Keystone is another prime additive to customize your van (courtesy Keystone).

285

If you own a mini that features front-wheel drive, you must give consideration to wheel offset requirements. This can vary on front-wheel drive vehicles (see Chapter 20).

The Cragar "Quick Trick" is a fine chrome and matte mag featuring the popular modular perforated wheel (Fig. 24-3). A similar offering is produced by Keystone designated the Solar-10 (Fig. 24-4). Rocket promotes its White Mod and RB11 simulated spoke pattern shown in Fig. 24-5.

Superior's modular perforated Monte Carlo (Fig. 24-6) is another worthy minivan wheel contender. The ultra-sophisticated custom buff will opt for the Superior California Wire, superior in quality as well as price (Fig. 24-7).

Chrysler's Direct Connection offers a complete line of Shelby custom wheels for front-wheel drive cars and minivans. Figure 24-8 shows the Reversed Daytona and simulated wire mags.

Those of you not wanting to go the mag wheel route, which may stretch your budget, can avail themselves of custom hubcaps. These greatly enhance the appearance of stock wheels.

Del-Met, a company specializing in superior quality hubcaps, feature a full line of dynamite mag and wire simulated hubcaps that will stand up appearance-wise to many contemporary mag wheels. Del-Met features over a hundred styles, including wire-spoked caps that are breathtaking. Del-Met also offers wheel cover locks to counter hubcap ripoffs.

The Del-Met line is stylish and economical; a recommended

Fig. 24-5. A simulated spoke pattern is shown in the White Mod (left) and RB II (right) by Rocket.

Fig. 24-6. Superior's modular perforated Monte Carlo (courtesy Superior Industries).

Fig. 24-7. The California wire will appeal to the sophisticated custom buff in quality as well as price (courtesy Superior Industries International).

Fig. 24-8. Shelby custom wheels featuring the Reversed Daytona (right) and simulated wire mags (left) (courtesy Direct Connection, Chrysler).

alternate route to custom wheel decor. A catalog to cover all of their wheel cover offerings may be obtained by writing:

Del-Met Corp.
44 West Street
Walton, NY 13856

A number of you may want to add your own seats and accessories to glorify your minis. Two good sources for everything "vanny" are:

Van Mart of California
11700 E. Washington Bl.
Whittier, CA 90606

Sporty Parts
55479 Lexington Park Drive
Elkhart, IN

Sources and locations of van conversion and accessory houses are included in the nationwide Van Conversion Directory in the Appendix.

Appendix

Van Conversion Directory

ABC Enterprises, Inc.
8905 Mentor Avenue
Mentor, OH 44060
216/255-5211

Action Vans
2727 E. Avalon Avenue
Muscle Shoals, AL 35660
205/383-7820

Advantage Corporation
516 E. Madison Street
Goshen, IN 46526
219/534-2694

Advantage Vans
901 Clark Street
Stevens Point, WI 54481
715/341-2712

Aero Leisure Industries
1601 West 25th Street
Kansas City, MO 64108
816/842-3611

A&J Vans
333 Washington Street
Valders, WI 54245
414/775-4694

American Car & Van
111 Slaton Highway
Lubbock, TX 79404
806/745-5556

American Van
15181 Telegraph
Detroit, MI 48239
313/255-6226

American Van Conv.
5601-A Rosedale Hwy.
Bakersfield, CA 93308
805/327-4134

Anaheim Vans
616 23rd St.
Houston, TX 77008
713/868-6147

Barrows Enterp.
1924 Washington Blvd.
Comanche, IA 52730
319/259-8391

BDR Vehicles
2915 Cooper
Arlington, TX 76015
817/467-9250

Beachcomber Vans, Inc.
3300 W. Capitol Ave.
W. Sacramento, CA 95691

Bentley Corp.
P.O. Drawer 464
Grandview, TX 76050
817/866-2611

Bivouac Industries
P.O. Box 125
Cassopolis, MI 49031

Bivouac Industries
P.O. Box 279
Vandalia, MI 49095
616/476-9794

Black Hawk Vans
Oak St. & Hwy 79
Black Hawk, SD 57718
605/787-4975

Blue Bird Body Co.
P.O. Box 937
Fort Valley, GA 31030
912/825-2021

Braun Corp.
1014 S. Monticello
Winamac, IN 46996
219/946-6157

Bremen Motor Corp.
425 Industrial Drive
Bremen, IN 46506
219/546-3791

Broughman Industries
14320 Ramona Ave.
Chino, CA 91710
714/597-1893

Cammilot Conversions
5401 S.W. 31st Ave.
Ocala, FL 32670
904/351-8860

Camp Mobile Vans
5402 Pine Park St.
Schofield, WI 54476
715/359-4709

Capitol Vans
1819 Roosevelt Court
Arlington, TX 76013
817/469-6688

Cardinal Conversions
1400 Wilmington
Washington, OH 43160
614/335-2707

Care Van Conversions
54784 Beech Road
Osceola, IN 46561
219/259-6932

Carefree Caravans
4508 E. 27th St.
Kansas City, MO 64127
816/921-1195

Cargo Master
P.O. Box 724
Goshen, IN 46526
219/875-8542

Carrera Designs, Inc.
2510 Middlebury
Elkhart, IN 46514
219/294-7174

Carriage, Inc.
P.O. Box 246, Hwy 13
Millersburg, IN 46543
219/642-3622

Cars & Concepts, Inc.
12500 E. Grand River Ave.
Brighton, MI 48116
313/227-9300

Cavalier Vans
2732-38 S.E. Loop 820
Ft. Worth, TX 76140
817/551-5890

Centurion-Lehman, Inc.
P.O. Box 645
Sturgis, MI 49091
616/651-4728

Century Motor Coach Co.
53387 Ada Drive
Elkhart, IN 46514
219/262-1511

Champion Home Bldrs. Co.
5573 North Street
Dryden, MI 48428
313/796-2211

Champion RV's
P.O. Box 1287
Elkhart, IN 46515
219/522-7385

Chaparral Vans
937 S. Laredo
San Antonio, TX 78204
512/222-8546

Chariot Vans, Inc.
210 Kraus St.
Edwardsburg, MI 49112
616/663-3615

Chef's Campers, Inc.
1425 N.W. Ballard Way
Seattle, WA 98107
206/783-2700

Chenelle Motorvans, Ltd.
30034 County Road 10
Elkhart, IN 46514
219/264-0631

Choo Choo Systems
2205 Polymer Dr.
Chattanooga, TN 37421
615/899-5382

Citation Motor Coach Corp.
25786 Miner Road
Elkhart, IN 46515
219/262-3484

Classic Manuf.
208 N. Sentry Dr.
Mansfield, TX 76063
817/477-2606

Classic Vans
Box 508
Faulkton, SD 57438
605/598-4437

Coachland, Inc.
3361 Lansing Road
Charlotte, MI 48813
517/645-7474

Coachmen Industries
State Road 13 N
Middlebury, IN 46540
219/825-5821

Colorado Freedom Wheels
10880 LeRoy Drive
North Glen, CO 80233
303/457-3312

Companion Vans, Inc.
Box 148
Kosciusko, MS 39090
601/289-7711

Companion Vans, Inc.
Blue Bonnett Ind. Park
McGregor, TX 76657
817/840-3271

Concept Editions, Inc.
26560 Windsor Ave.
Elkhart, IN 46514
219/264-9591

Consolidated Leisure Ind.
1100 Woodlawn Ave.
Elkhart, IN 46515
219/262-4521

Contec, Inc.
924 Williams St.
Lake Geneva, WI 53147
414/248-3291

Contemp Campers
11611 Cantara St.
North Hollywood, CA 91605
213/768-2800

Contemporary Coach Co.
64654 U.S. 33 St.
Goshen, IN 46526
219/533-4161

Continental Van & Body
56183 Ash Road
Osceola, IN 46561
219/674-5175

Conversions by Cimmarron
57780 County Road #105
Elkhart, IN 46515
219/295-5054

Coons Mfg. Co.
15730 S. 169 Hwy.
Olathe, KS 66061
913/764-5665

Country Compact
P.O. Box 608
Jay, OK 74346
918/253-4832

Country Cruiser, Inc.
2206 Toledo Road
Elkhart, IN 46514
219/522-7586

Country Roads
775 Barber
Athens, Georgia 30601
404/353-8267

Crescent City Customs, Inc.
2424 Hickory Ave.
Metairie, LA 70003
504/738-2634

CTI/Geneva, Inc.
904 Maxwell St.
Lake Geneva, WI 53147
414/248-0244

Custom Camp Vans
12155 Magnolia #6B
Riverside, CA 92503
714/359-3443

Custom Coachworks
1309 E. Walnut St.
Sioux Falls, SD 57103
605/334-5339

Custom Craft Vans, Inc.
960 W. Armour Ave.
Milwaukee, WI 53221
414/744-8118

Custom Creations
2808 Pendleton Ave.
Anderson, IN 46011
317/649-0504

Custom Fit of Texas
P.O. Box 539
Decatur, TX 76234
817/627-5916

Custom Vans
4628 North "E" St.
Lansing, MI 48906
517/482-2116

Custom Van Enterprises
20932 Harper St.
Harper Woods, MI 48224
313/886-8755

Custom Vans of Utah
3665 S. 300 West
Salt Lake City, UT 84115
801/266-1552

Day Cruiser
22828 Pine Creek Road
Elkhart, IN 46515
219/293-1513

D'Elegance
1320 S. Merrifield
Mishawaka, IN 46544
219/256-0265

Delta Two Van Conversions
54635 County Road 17
Elkhart, IN 46514
219/293-4418

Delta Van Conversions
52652 Mobile Drive
Elkhart, IN 46515
219/262-4621

Designer Coach Div of A&S
435 West Harrison St.
Elkhart, IN 46516
219/293-8696

Diamond Van Company
State Road 15
Bristol, IN 46507
219/848-4329

Dimensions Vans
Rt. 1 Box 459P
Homossassa, FL 32646
904/795-5125

Disco Vans
812 N. McKenzie St.
Foley, AL 36535
205/943-1808

DMC Div. of DM Conversions
12401 66th St. N
Largo, FL 33543
813/530-3691

DMC Div. of DM Conversions
12651 W. Silver Spring Dr.
Butler, WI 53007
414/781-1170

DMR Van Conversions
204 Cedar St.
Monticello, IA 52310
319/465-5620

Dodgen Industries
Highway 169 North
Humboldt, IA 50548
515/332-3755

Durango Coach Corp.
17140 S. Kingsview Ave.
Carson, CA 90746
213/516-6662

Eastern Turtle Top
10822-B Woodsboro Road
Woodsboro, MD 21798
301/845-8070

El Dorado RV, Inc.
1200 W. Tenth
Minneapolis, KS 67467
913/392-2174

Elk Enterprises, Inc.
25771 Miner Road
Elkhart, IN 46515
219/264-0768

Elkhart Motor Car Co.
27895 County Road 10 W
Elkhart, IN 46514
219/262-3561

Esquire, Inc.
Route 1, Box 19925-M205
Edwardsburg, MI 49112
616/641-5194

Etnom Corp.
25954 Pierina Dr.
Elkhart, IN 46514
219/262-4411

E-Vans, Inc.
3505 Brooklyn Ave.
Fort Wayne, IN 46809
219/747-7452

Excalibur Vans of Texas
2800 West Division
Arlington, TX 76012
817/265-3943

Exclusive Manufacturing Co.
2501 Arkansas Lane
Grand Prairie, TX 75051
214/988-1822

Executive Ind., Inc.
5500 East LaPalma
Anaheim, Ca 92807
714/524-8640

Expand A Van
100 F. Cristich Lane
Campbell, CA 95008
408/377-7120

Explorer Vans
P.O. Box 213
Warsaw, IN 46580
219/267-7666

Family Vans, Inc.
730 Airport Road
Lakewood, NJ 08701
201/370-1022

Fiberlite Campers
8585 Mentor Avenue
Mentor, OH 44060
216/942-6938

Fleetwood Enterp., Inc.
2970 Myers St.
Riverside, CA 92523
714/785-3788

Fleetwood Enterp., Inc.
RFD#1 Route 487
Paxinos, PA 17860
717/644-0817

Foxey Vans, Inc.
2300 Town Street
Pensacola, FL 32505
904/438-3133

Free Wheel Vans
16002 W 4th Avenue
Golden, CO 80401
303/278-2972

Frontier Vans
1325 William Tate Blvd
Grapevine, TX 76051
817/481-6250

Galaxy Vans
3570 N. State Road 7
Hollywood, FL

Galaxy Vans
Highway 18 East
Algona, IA 50511
515/295-2802

Galles Vans
1709 Peyco Drive N
Arlington, TX 76017
800/722-8832

Geering Luxury Vans
17090 State Road 120E
Bristol, IN 46507
219/848-7602

Georgie Boy Mfg. Inc.
Industrial Park
Edwardsburg, MI 49112
616/663-3835

Ger-Win Vans, Inc.
807 S. Division St.
Bristol, IN 46507-0578
219/848-7642

Ger-Win Vans of Kansas
15365 South Keeler
Olathe, KS 66062
913/782-7579

Gladiator, Inc.
55135 County Road 1
Elkhart, IN 46515
219/262-2633

Glastop Inc.
429 S. Dixie Hwy
Pompano Beach, FL
305/781-8460

Good Times Vans
Farm Road & Hwy 110
Grandview, TX 76050
817/866-2611

Granada Conver., Inc.
19901 County Road 8
Bristol, IN 46507
219/848-7446

Gran Prix, Ltd.
2417 Oakland Ave.
Elkhart, IN 46517
219/295-6131

Gran Prix Van Conver.
1581 93rd Lane
Blaine, MN 55434
612-786-7801

Gran-Ville Delta Two, Inc.
54635 County Road 17 S
Elkhart, IN 46515
219/293-4418

Happy Times, Inc.
RR 13 Box 806 HT
Fort Meyers, FL 33908
813/482-2700

Helper Ind. of Mid South
5444 Lamar Avenue
Memphis, TN 38118
901/365-6460

Heritage Rec. Vehicles
13065 Anderson Road
Granger, IN 46530
219/272-8990

Holiday Rambler Corp.
65528 State Road 19 N
Wakarusa, IN 46573
219/862-7211

International Vehicles, Cor.
200 Legion Street
Bristol, IN 46507
219/848-7686

Ivory Coach Co.
407 Beltline
Dallas, TX 75253
214/286-1970

Jackson Classic Vans
4104 Paige Street
Michigan Ctr, MI 49254
517/764-5811

Jade Van Conversions
903 N. Nappanee
Elkhart, IN 46514
219/264-7473

Jayco, Inc.
58075 St. Road 13 S
Middlebury, IN 46540
219/825-5861

Johnson Conversions
R.R. 1 US 6 E
Nappanee, IN 46550
219/773-7273

Keenan World of Cust.
P.O. Box 854
Mauldin, SC 29662
803/297-1886

Kellogg Manuf, Inc.
59140 County Rd 3 S
Elkhart, IN 46517
219/295-4194

Kentron, Inc.
52897 Dexter Drive
Elkhart, IN 46514
219/262-3861

Kingfisher Vans
Box 777
King Fisher, OK 73750
405/375-5766

Klein Kustom Koach Co.
3653-A Trousdale
Nashville, TN 37204
615/833-6777

Komfort Koach, Inc.
5202 Crittendon Drive
Louisville, KY 40213
502/368-1633

Komfort Koach, Inc.
2811 Watterson Trail
Louisville, KY 40299
502/267-4201

K & S Conversions
521 East Lincoln
Goshen, IN 46546
219/534-3637

Kustom Fit. Mfg. Co.
100 Industrial Avenue
Pioneer, OH 43554
419/737-2314

Kustom Fit. Mfg. Co.
1601 S Church St.
Decatur, TX 76234
817/627-5916

Kustom Kar & Van
P.O. Box 296
Cook, NE 68329
402/864-5811

LA Industries, Inc.
Sach's Industrial Park
28722 Jami Drive
Elkhart, IN 46517
219/293-4614

L&D Manuf. Inc.
P.O. Box 599
Sturgis, Michigan 49001
616/651-4728

Lakeside Convers.
25600 N. Shore Rd.
Elkhart, IN 46514
219/264-5271

Land Yachts
1624 Waurika St.
Elkhart, IN 46516
219/295-5613

Lands Design, Inc.
42645 Thorne Drive
Elkhart, IN 46517
219/262-2567

LaTour Luxury Vans
794 S Broadway
Hicksville, NY 11801
516/681-3648

La-Van Convers.
4817 N 56th St.
Lincoln, NE 68504
402/467-3534

Lazt N Campers
RR #1 Hwy 121
Warrensburg, IL 62573
217/652-3281

Legacy Vans
22932 Pine Creek Rd.
Elkhart, IN 46514
219/293-7040

Leisure Editions, East
255 S Whitford Rd
Exton, PA 19341
215/524-0570

Leisure Vans, Inc.
52705 Thorne Drive
Elkhart, IN 46514
219/262-4561

LeVan Specialty Co.
14923 Proctor Ave.
Industry, CA 91746
213/968-6555

Lipps Industries, Inc.
P.O. Box 415
Bristol, IN 46517
219/848-7618

Longview Van Corp.
1147 Center Street
Elkhart, IN 46514
219/295-4277

LRP of Wisconsin
501 East Centralia
Elkhorn, WI 53121
414/723-6700

Luxury Cruiser
52906 Dexter Drive
Elkhart, IN 46514
219/264-9671

Luxury Vans
P.O. Box 105
Keene, TX 76059
817/465-7796

Luxury Vans of Elkhart
2525 Warren Street
Elkhart, IN 46516
219/295-4355

Magna Van
5330 66th St. N
St. Petersburg, FL 33709
813/544-9433

Mark III Conversions
2935 NW 8th Ave.
Ocala, FL 32678
904/732-5878

Marque, Inc.
64654 US Hwy 33
Goshen, IN 46526
219/533-4164

Mastercraft Vans
P.O. Box 349
Goshen, In 46553
219/533-1664

Medallion Coach
524 S. Main
Middlebury, IN 46540
219/825-2171

Melody Coach Ind.
2830 Gallows Road
Vienna, VA 22180
703/560-6200

Metro Van, Inc.
1730 Markle Avenue
Elkhart, IN 46517
219/522-3990

Midas Van Convers.
1520 Mishawaka Street
Elkhart, IN 46515
219/262-3474

Midway Truck & Coach
29391 West 33rd
Elkhart, IN 46514
219/262-4581

Mobile Traveler
P.O. Box 258
Junction City, KS 66441
913/238-7176

Mobility Ind., Inc.
37555 Willow Street
Newark, CA 94560
415/794-6441

National Coach Corp.
130 West Victoria Blvd.
Gardena, CA 94560
213/538-3122

National Traveler
2142 W. Broad St.
Athens, CA 30604
404/353-1572

Newmar Industries
P.O. Box 30
Nappanee, IN 46550
219/773-7791

NuConcepts, Inc.
27887 Wade Drive
Elkhart, IN 46514
219/264-9554

NuWa Industries, Inc.
Box 768
Chanute, KS 66720
316/431-2088

O.C. Conversions, Inc.
9914 Oakland Drive
Kalamazoo, MI 49002
616/323-0160

O'Neill Enterprises, Inc.
P.O. Box 111
Twin Lakes, WI 53181
414/877-9220

Ozzo Coach, Inc.
RR #3 Box 33A
Albertsville, AL 35940
205/878-2399

Panda Vans
125 North Madison
Greentown, IN 46936
317/457-6781

Paratransit Vehicle Mfg. Co.
400 N Nappanee St.
Elkhart, IN 46515
219/295-6249

Premier Editions, Inc.
27801 Dexter Drive
Elkhart, IN 46514
219/262-4477

Prestige Vans
23580 Stonehedge
Novi, MI 48050
313/477-9564

Quality Coaches, Inc.
3200 Middlebury
Elkhart, IN 46514
219/293-0568

Red-E-Kamp, Inc.
Mira Loma Space Ctr.
Mira Loma, CA 91752
714/685-0151

Redmont RV's
Red Bay, AL 35582
205/356-9595

Regency Vans
Highway 411 N
Cartersville, GA 30120
404/382-8381

Ritz Company
P.O. Box 7190
Phoenix, AZ 85011
602/957-0692

Riviera Vans, Inc.
P.O. Box 563
Goshen, IN 46526

RoadRunner Vans
809 S Sherman
Richardson, TX 75081
214/783-8155

Rockwood, Inc.
201 West Elm St.
Millersburg, IN 4653
219/642-3313

Roll-A-Long Vans, Inc.
210 E Crowther St
Placentia, CA 92670
714/528-9600

Roman Wheels, Inc.
State Road 15 S
Bristol, IN 46507
219/848-7646

Santa Fe Vans
1801 Minnie Street
Elkhart, IN 46516
219/293-0585

Roman Wheels South, Inc.
5454 W Crenshaw St.
Tampa, FL 33614
813/886-2184

Seven-O-Seven Ind., Inc.
2625 Lowell
Elkhart, IN 46517
219/294-6151

Royal Coach of Texas
204 Texas Avenue
Round Rock, TX 78664
512/244-1616

Sherrod Vans, Inc.
6464 Greenland Road
Jacksonville, FL 32203
904/268-3321

Rusco Van Conversions
Box 2453
Denton, TX 76201
817/382-1568

Shuttlecraft, Inc.
P.O. Box 751
Pell City, AL 35125
205/338-9401

RVC, Inc.
1701 Century Drive
Goshen, IN 46526
219/534-2424

Signature Van Corp.
28951 U.S. 20 West
Elkhart, IN 46514
219/295-2530

Sandpiper Van Corp.
108 S Elkhart Ave.
Elkhart, IN 46514
219/294-7664

Skyline Corp.
2520 ByPass Road
Elkhart, IN 46515
219/294-7457

Sands Industries, Inc.
52161 U.S. #131
Three Rivers, MI 49093
616/273-8441

Smith's Van Convers.
5010 South M-106
Stockbridge, MI 49285
517/851-8103

San Kar Vans
1401 W. 40 Hwy
Blue Springs, MO 64015
816/229-8888

Smitty's Vans
401 Commercial
Belton, MO 64012
816/331-3007

Sonday's Vans
9230 120th Ave.
Kenosha, WI 53142
414/857-7933

Southeastern Mobility Co.
P.O. Box 104
Philadelphia, TN 37846
615/458-4661

Southern Coach of Grensboro
406 Pine Street
Grensboro, NC 27401
919/378-0567

Southern Comfort Vans
322 W. Harrison
Elkhart, IN 46516
219/522-5772

Southern Motor Coach Co.
301 Jimmy Daniel Road
Bogart, GA 30622
404/353-2210

Specialized Vehicles
58190 County Rd 3 South
Elkhart, IN 46517
219/295-1214

Sportscoach of America
1100 N. Woodlawn
Elkhart, IN 46515
219/262-3471

Sportscraft, Inc.
57978 County Road 3
Elkhart, IN 46517
219/522-3475

Sportsmobile, Inc.
250 Court Street
Huntington, IN 46750
219/356-5435

Sportsmobile, Inc.
9805B Gray Blvd
Austin, TX 78758
512/835-4409

Stagecoach VIP, Inc.
3504 Dickerson Road
Nashville, TN 37207
615/868-6681

Star Coach
55265 County Road 3
Elkhart, IN 46514
219/295-1455

Starcraft Company
West Michigan Street
Topeka, IN 46571
219/593-2550

Starline Corp.
Highway 22 East
Wellman IA 52356
319/646-2964

Starline Van Company
Box 95 1001 E. Main
Albion, IN 46701
219/636-3110

Star Truk
Route 18
Transfer, PA 16154
412/646-1789

Stimus Van Convers.
123 Princess Way
Granger, IN 46530
219/277-5092

Studebaker Motor Coach, Inc.
P.O. Box 4248
South Bend, IN 46634
219/234-4010

Sun Belt Vans
P.O. Box 207
Kosciusko, MI 39090
601/289-1917

TEC Recreational Vehicles
Box 512
Goshen, IN 46526
219/533-4161

Tech Trans, Inc.
17090 State Rd 120 E
Bristol, IN 46507
219/848-7655

Thomas Built Buses, Inc.
P.O. Box 2450
High Point, NC 27261
919/889-4871

Tidwell Touring Coach Co.
P.O. Box 428
Haleyville, AL 35565
205/486-9583

Together Custom Vans
141 East Busch Blvd.
Tampa, FL 33612
813/932-9327

Toyota Motor Sales USA
19001 S Western Ave.
Torrance, CA 90509
213/618-4578

Trail Wagons, Inc.
1100 E. Lincoln Avenue
Yakima, WA 98907
509/248-9026

Tram Body & Coach
5150 1-70
St. Charles, MO 63301
314/441-4020

Trans-Aire Intern.
52652 Mobile Drive
Elkhart, IN 46515
219/262-3411

Tra Tech Corp/Midwest
3801 Industrial
Pontiac, MI 48057
313/852-2620

Tra Tech Corp/National
7334 Tower Street
Fort Worth, TX 76118
817/595-0305

Tra Tech Corp/Southeast
1075 South Cobb Drive
Marietta, GA 30060
404/427-2500

TravelCraft, Inc.
1135 Kent Street
Elkhart, IN 46514
219/262-4651

Travel Equipment Corp.
P.O. Box 512
Goshen, IN 46526
219/533-4161

Travel Master Vans
414 West Fork
Arlington, TX 76012
817/261-7943

Travel Quest, Inc.
Loop 304 South
Crockett, TX 75835
409/544-2175

Trix Mfg. Co.
500 W Irving Park Rd.
Bensenville, IL 60106
312/595-6340

Turtle Top, Inc.
502 NW 75th Street
Gainesville, FL 32607
904/377-8755

Turtle Top, Inc.
118 West LaFayette
Goshen, IN 46526
219/533-4116

Unique Vans, Inc.
12009 South Cicero
Alsip, IL 60658
312/597-5265

Universal/Mid-Atlantic
1900 Hanover Pike
Hampstead, MD 21074
301/374-5000

Universal Motor Coach
810 Broadus
Sturgis, MI 49091
616/651-4756

U.S. Conversions, Inc.
27861 Dexter Drive
Elkhart, IN 46514
219/262-3681

Utilimaster Corp.
65266 State Road 19
Wakarusa, IN 46573
219/862-7400

Valley Vans, Inc.
11920 County Road 14
Middlebury, IN 46540
219/825-9411

Van Aire
53293 Marina
Elkhart, IN 46515
219/262-4557

Van America, Inc.
1402 Lincoln Way, E
Goshen, IN 46526
219/534-1418

Van Attic, Inc.
4554 Gravois
St. Louis, MO 63116
314/352-4554

Van Barn
22 S 20th St.
Battle Creek, MI 49015
616/968-7141

Van Camp Industries
8184 Alpine Avenue
Sacramento, CA 95826
916/452-3441

Van Convers, by Carriage
P.O. Box 246
Millersburg, IN 46543
219/642-3622

Van Convers, by Kogon
1524 Springhill Dr.
McLean, VA 22102
703-821-6950

Van Epoch, Inc.
15055 32 Mile Road
romero, MI 48065
313/237-0554

Van Epoch, Inc.
56120 Van Dyke Ave.
Washington, MI 49084
313/781-6771

Van Express
26536 County Road 7
Elkhart, IN 46514
219/264-9658

VanGo, Inc.
P.O. Box 81
Nappanee, IN 46550
219/773-2655

Van House
1801 Cushman Drive
Lincoln, NE 68512
402/423-3600

Van-C
6010 West 10th St.
Greeley, CO 80631
303/353-1002

Van Masters Division of
Colamco, Inc.
1529 Alum Creek Dr.
Columbus OH 43209
614/253-0627

Van One
55955 Hoosier
Mishawaka, IN 46545
219/255-4432

Varsity Vehicles
127 Dividend Court
Arlington, TX 76012
817/277-9500

Vehicle Concepts Corp.
Bristol Ind. Park
Bristol, IN 46507
219/988-7494

Vemco Builders, Inc.
P.O. Box 1305
Elkhart, IN 46515
219/293-4527

Viking Vans
R.R. 3 Box 10A
Flandreau, SD 57028
605/997-2427

Vista Mfg. Co.
27969 County Road 6
Elkhart, IN 46514
219/264-0711

V.P.O. Corp.
2118 By Pass Road
Elkhart, IN 46515
219/295-3150

Waldoch Crafts, Inc.
13821 Lake Drive
Forest Lake, MN 55025
612/464-3215

Wieland Designs, Inc.
901 East Madison
Goshen, IN 46526
219/533-2168

Windsor Motor Vans, Inc.
1400 Spencer Road
Newton, KS 67114
316/284-2324

Winnebago Industries, Inc.
P.O. Box 152
Forest City, IA 50436
515/582-3535

Wright Carriage Co.
P.O. Box 604
Ashburn, GA 31714
912/567-9597

Wynona Van Convers.
1760 Cheyenne
Nappanee, IN 46550
219/773-4972

Xplorer Motor Home Div.
Frank Industries
3950 Burnsline Road
Brown City, MI 48416
313/346-2771

Zimmer Motor Vans
2801 13th Ave. East
Cordele, GA 33060
912/273-5320

Zodiac Vans
P.O. Box 157
Galena, KS 66739
316/783-5041

Index